Praise for the Book

The eight stories in this book are very inspiring and challenging and I am sure it would help other budding entrepreneurs to be innovative and creative.

Anu Aga
Ex-Chairperson, *Thermax Ltd.*

Corporations need to come together to support new ideas that identify problems, devise solutions and create new segments in the market.

Ashwin Dani
Non-Executive Chairman, *Asian Paints Ltd.*

Innovative thinking by young India holds the key to improve lives and uplift communities. When larger companies lend them genuine support, stories of success such as these get told.

Gautam Mago
General Partner, *A91 Partners*

Indian entrepreneurs have shown unique creativity and frugal innovation to solve India-specific problems, and in the process have shown the path to entrepreneurs in other parts of the world addressing similar challenges. Their learnings summarized here will drive next-level innovation, competency and impact!

Sandeep Singhal
Director, *SEDEMAC Technologies*

Bold and disruptive innovations can accelerate the pace of progress and enable positive impact. The stories of these brave innovators are truly inspirational.

Hari Menon
India Country Director, *Bill & Melinda Gates Foundation*

Timely funding, mentorship, a supportive network—all contribute to the entrepreneurial ecosystem and drive social impact while delivering financial returns. These success stories are a testament to the commendable effort by all stakeholders.

Roopa Kudva
Managing Director, *Omidyar Network India*

A wealth of experiences, insights and innovations! It makes the journey of an innovator, relatable and attainable and also gives sharp insights along the way. I would recommend this read to anyone but especially the next generation of innovators the country is nurturing.

Rajiv Bajaj
Managing Director, *Bajaj Auto Ltd.*

Understanding and getting excited by the challenges of others, getting motivated by their success, trying to cultivate their qualities must be stirring. This book is a compass for such budding innovators who seek to navigate through the volatile marketplace that is today.

Harsha Bhogle
TV Commentator/Presenter

Scaling up is a challenge that most start-ups face. This book gives you a useful framework on how to do this successfully. And real life stories of those who have successfully done it, using technology and innovation.

Sam Balsara
Chairman, *Madison World*

This book narrates many stories of challenges, perseverance and growth in each stage. Will be very relatable and inspiring for young entrepreneurs!

Prof Sujatha Ramdorai
Professor and Canada Research Chair,
University of British Columbia, Canada

Our country is in dire need of innovative solutions across spheres and nurturing ecosystems and encouraging innovators to succeed will build a vibrant India. This book shows us many glimpses of that.

Amit Chandra
Chairman, *Bain Capital India Office*

India's success depends on inspiring and enabling millions of people to tinker, invent, solve local problems and start businesses some of which become big. These inspiring stories show 'ordinary' people can do extraordinary things thereby changing our world.

Ravi Venkatesan
Chairman, *Bank of Baroda*

The market is in a state of disequilibrium, making continuous innovation the need of the hour. A supportive ecosystem can build a risk appetite towards that end as you will find in this book.

Rajeev Bakshi
Non-Executive & Independent Director,
Marico Ltd.

7 SUTRAS OF INNOVATION

7 SUTRAS OF INNOVATION

STORIES OF SCALE-UPS THAT ARE TRANSFORMING INDIA

NIKHIL INAMDAR

WITH **MARICO INNOVATION FOUNDATION**

FOREWORD BY
HARSH MARIWALA

JAICO PUBLISHING HOUSE

Ahmedabad Bangalore Bhopal Chennai
Delhi Hyderabad Kolkata Lucknow Mumbai

Published by Jaico Publishing House
A-2 Jash Chambers, 7-A Sir Phirozshah Mehta Road
Fort, Mumbai - 400 001
jaicopub@jaicobooks.com
www.jaicobooks.com

7 SUTRAS OF INNOVATION
ISBN 978-93-89305-25-8

First Jaico Impression: 2020

Page design and layout:
Special Effects Graphics Design Company, Mumbai

Foreword

Starting Marico has been an experience of self-discovery and growth as much as it has been one of success and insights. From the modest lanes of Masjid Bunder in Mumbai to becoming one of India's best-known Fast-Moving Consumer Goods (FMCG) brands was not by accident, of course, but it was not the end goal either. For me, what remained a focal point at every stage of growth was homing in on what was important at that particular moment in time and letting enough of those moments accumulate to ultimately create the value that we see manifested today. It has also not been an individual journey, but a collective commitment of those who joined hands with us along the way in order to share our vision of making a difference and continually innovate to deliver excellence to our end consumer and our teams. This is what has helped us create a right to win at every juncture in our journey and as a team we remain steadfast about reinforcing it by keeping a few principles front and center at all times.

If I had one advice to give to any innovator or entrepreneur from what I have learnt and observed over the years, it is that the only assured way to emerge among the front-runners over the long term is to remain innovative and to focus on putting one foot in front of the other while remaining curious and strategic about what lies ahead.

Remaining aware and open to new possibilities while focusing on the goal at hand is essential to building an innovative organization. Additionally, what makes a successful organization is the culture that binds its people, and it is necessarily something that the leadership must drive with rigor. At Marico, our culture has a few key tenets, one that encourages risk-taking, does not punish failures and rewards resourcefulness. We also create spaces for people to share, ideate and collaborate deliberately, to ensure the underlying pulse of the organization continues to beat with innovative thinking and approaches. It could be an idea that fills a gap and creates value, a different way of doing things, or a pioneering approach to solving a crucial problem. Innovation is what gives an enterprise a definitive competitive advantage.

While the concept is often viewed from a business lens, increasingly I find that innovation is taking place in nearly every aspect of life, including in the creation of meaningful social impact. This is important for a country like India where the public delivery of basic human needs such as education, healthcare and sanitation require radical disruption. It is heartening to note that alongside commercial success, Indian organizations are making a significant contribution to create social impact by leveraging the power of innovation.

A steady improvement in the country's position on the Global Innovation Index (GII) bears testament to the fact. From ranking 81 among 126 economies in 2015, we have inched up to the 57th mark in 2018—a quick ascent by all means. Alongside the birth of disruptive new start-ups across commercial domains such as e-commerce, logistics and e-mobility, the country has become home to many laudable innovators who are playing an increasingly important role to develop solutions which address real-world problems that the nation grapples with.

India is evolving fast to improve the quality of innovation that comes out of its private sector firms and start-ups, leaving the reverse-engineered 'jugaad' tag far behind. Indigenous innovation coming out of India is seeing the light of day as more companies weave innovation into the fabric of their organizational culture as well as the products or services they put out for the end consumer to simplify their lives or enhance their quality in some manner.

This is an exciting new chapter in the history of our nation, and this book features remarkable companies that straddle both the business and social domains. It is the second in the series of books on innovation being brought out by Marico Innovation Foundation (MIF).

In 2009, MIF released the first book—*Making Breakthrough Innovations Happen.* It distilled and dissected some of the thought processes that inspired 11 organizations to achieve quantum innovation in their industries by turning established norms upside down and pulling off the impossible in their fields. It was a deep dive into how innovation happens within a given set-up. It addressed some critical questions: Can an organization be innovative with a legacy mindset? Can new challengers take on established giants through their entrepreneurial vision? Do organizations need to set orbit-shifting challenges in order to make a dent? Through carefully delineated case studies the book explored these questions in an eminently readable, non-academic format, setting a benchmark and selling more than 65,000 copies and becoming a bestseller in the genre.

This one, though not a sequel, is a logical successor, and an extension of the themes that preoccupied us in the first. But it sharpens focus on the question of scale.

Despite steady progress in our ability to innovate, the rate of failure among start-ups in India reveals an urgent need for mentoring to address the challenges faced and help the nation's entrepreneurs join the big league of innovative nations. This is where deconstructing the success of the entrepreneurs who have crossed these roadblocks, and understanding how they got to the crucial inflection point could prove insightful.

Having survived the start-up phase, the next challenge to surmount is the ambition to scale up. What does it really take for an idea to scale? How do you sustain good innovation and grow an idea from seed to size without being scathed?

Scaling up requires a rigorous, execution-related mindset and an ability to juggle multiple balls at one go, but not all great inventors are necessarily great entrepreneurs, which is why not all great ideas translate into great companies.

Are there universal principles that scale-ups abide by? Can they provide cross-learnings to other start-ups as they get on to the path to scale? These are some of the questions this book hopes to address through real-life cases and lived experiences of entrepreneurs who have successfully scaled up. It features eight markedly diverse companies hailing from the Indian business start-up and non-profit universe. Over the years MIF has closely watched and worked with them to solve critical business challenges so that they can pole vault and not just leapfrog their innovation to scale. They have all now reached a tipping point in their business journeys where they may not yet be organizations that have reached critical mass but have undoubtedly set the groundwork for taking that final leap into the big league, surmounting the very real barriers to scale.

Their entrepreneurial journeys featured here are not only deeply inspiring at a human level but also provide valuable insights that other start-ups can use to put themselves on the elevator to scale.

There is much to learn here. Happy reading!

Harsh Mariwala
Founder, Marico Innovation Foundation
& Chairman, Marico Ltd.

Preface

In 2003, Marico Innovation Foundation (MIF) was set up by Harsh Mariwala, a visionary leader with great foresight, who could already see the huge impact that innovation would have on our future. I have been intimately associated with MIF right from its birth. I have seen with pride how with the simple motto of 'inspire, impact and involve' it has been able to fuel innovation in India.

Two strategically conceived and executed flagship programs of MIF have been immensely successful.

The first is the MIF Awards which honour unheralded innovations impacting the community while showcasing inspiring exemplars for new generations of innovators. It has become one of India's pre-eminent biennial recognition platforms.

The second is the MIF Scale-Up Program which is an intensive mentorship program that guides innovative enterprises to solve critical business challenges. MIF thus helps in traversing the journey from invention to innovation, mind to marketplace, and most importantly, ideas to impact.

MIF does this by leading the winning innovations to relevant business and investment opportunities, providing access to industry stalwarts, imparting personalized training on the art of executive presence, powerful storytelling and spotlighting to a curated audience, etc.

MIF has been continuously raising the bar to ensure that the winners are those who alter the trajectory of business and society, not incrementally but disruptively by being not merely first to India but also to the world. Moreover, it has done so by not just following best practices but also creating next practices, and by not being exclusive to a privileged few but rather by being inclusive, thus making a difference for every Indian.

This book is a valuable addition to the global innovation knowledge base as it shows how eight MIF awardees, with enormous diversity in terms of sectors, products, business models and operations, have achieved results with speed, scale and sustainability. The book distils 'seven sutras' that were common to their successful journeys as they made the critical transition from 'childhood to adolescence'. These seven sutras are both powerful and universal.

I firmly believe that instead of remaining on the periphery innovation and entrepreneurship must be brought to the core in all our systems, including education. And when that happens, I have no doubt that this book will become the 'bible' to follow.

Dr. R. A. Mashelkar
Honorary Chairman, Governing Council,
Marico Innovation Foundation

A Note on Innovation

It was a pleasure to have been associated with this project and to write a few words for this second book by Marico Innovation Foundation.

Is innovation really increasing in the world? Is it too much of a buzzword? Why none from India or its mighty corporations? The truth is that buzz has value. Language and culture are hugely important in social transformation.

In Indian languages, there is no colloquial word for innovation. I emphasize colloquial—I know this because I speak Tamil, Hindi and Bengali fluently. There are words but you have to resort to an artifice. How and when did it come into English? The etymology of the word 'innovation' provides a clue. Canadian historian Benoit Godin states that the word first appeared in texts on law to mean renewing contracts. It had no connection with creativity, it merely meant renewal. During the seventeenth century, when Europe was far more conservative, every attempt to interpret religious matters was anathema. English Puritan Henry Burton published pamphlets against 'church innovators' to suggest that such people were upstarts and imitators—not very complimentary. 'Innovation' in the early years carried a negative tonal quality.

With the industrial revolution, invention became a highly desired activity and by 1800, the word came into common English usage. Google's Ngram database suggests that in 1800, the word 'invention' was used four times as frequently as innovation; after a century and a half, invention and innovation were used equally; and since 1970, innovation has overtaken invention and has been used more frequently. The distance between the usages of innovation and invention is increasing.

In the future, innovation will be more and more about scaling clever solutions to issues—about solving human problems with impact. And that is what this book is about.

Happy reading.

R. Gopalakrishnan
Author & Corporate Advisor, Member of the
Governing Council of Marico Innovation Foundation

Contents

Introduction

Scaling up a business is not quite the same thing as starting one. It is estimated that 70–90 percent of start-ups globally go kaput even before they are poised to make it big. It is a staggering statistic that screams for attention. Why do such few start-ups grow from seed to size? What is it exactly that makes scaling up pangs fatal for most entrepreneurs? And just what can enable more of them to cross the growth bridge with a higher success rate?

For entrepreneurs a business is really like their infant, and the journey—between start-up and scale-up—is quite akin to the treacherous ride between infancy and adolescence. It is riddled with health hazards that can prove risky to development in the absence of proper care and nutrition.

Scaling up too is all about providing your business with proper care and nutrition, i.e., building the capacity and capability to set it up on a high-performance path to growth. But if in child rearing, the focus is on right food, exercise, a good education, healthcare and an emotionally enriching environment to effect positive life outcomes and eliminate the risk of fatality, are there growing up strategies that early-stage businesses must employ in order to jump across the deep valley to scale and emerge unscathed? Are there universal rules that entrepreneurs and businessmen can apply as best practices to avoid the high failure rate that prevails among start-ups?

A good way to find out would be from innovators who have already traversed this perilous path, eliminated destructive behaviors that posed impediments to growth and created real value for their stakeholders.

Marico Innovation Foundation (MIF) was incepted in 2003 by Harsh Mariwala, the founder of Marico Ltd., to nurture entrepreneurship and innovation. Since 2006, MIF has been awarding a range of incredible companies operating in a cross section of industries in India for their game-changing innovations. These include for-profit enterprises, public sector undertakings and social impact organizations. Meticulously selected on the basis of a holistic evaluation process that considers parameters such as uniqueness of the concept, impact in sector of operation and potential scalability, these are companies that have passed a fine sieve.

Through the years, many of the awardees have generated significant impact with their innovations and garnered a degree of scale that makes them truly exceptional. No doubt, some have fallen by the wayside from a growth perspective and others have even run into troubled waters. But this book maps the success stories of the winners and gleans insights from their journeys with the hope that they will become a source of inspiration and knowledge for the wider business readership in India.

Irrespective of the fact that these companies represent divergent sectors, or that each of them have had their individual journeys and milestones that are not necessarily analogous with one another, they retain solid fundamental principles or sutras that emerge as common factorials in all of their scale-up stories.

This book covers eight awardees, each one dramatically different from the other in terms of its scope of operations, product profile, stage of growth, sector of function or business model. And yet, through this diversity, it has been possible to distill at least seven sutras of scaling up or universal principles that most of them have abided by in their individual journeys to success.

What are these?

1. Find a Gap in the Market and Create a Market in the Gap

Great start-ups usually have the ability to find gaps in the market that are not filled by existing products or services. Gaps are everywhere, but it takes a different vision to spot one and use it to your advantage. Sometimes it can happen purely as a matter of chance, on other occasions it could be a function of deep market research or carefully listening to customer feedback.

But finding a market gap is only half the battle won. While great importance is given to this knack, often not much attention is paid to a question that really determines whether a business can scale—is there a market in the gap that you can exploit or a capability to create one?

"The only thing worse than being wrong is being early," is an old truism that is greatly applicable to the start-up world. But ideas fail not only because they are way ahead of their time. Incapacity to monetize, lack of mature technology, inadequate customer base, poor execution and inability to maintain and expand a market position are among several reasons why great ideas do not scale.

Start-ups that have scaled are generally able to tick both boxes—they not only have an idea that is great but also the capability to map and create demand for it.

2. Be Firm But Flexible

This might sound like a dichotomy but it really is not. Companies that achieve scale successfully set clear goals for themselves, but keep evaluating and changing as they grow. They are steadfast in reaching their mission but quite flexible in the path they choose to reach there. Most of them develop unique growth models but follow the process of continuous learning and adapting.

Why is this so important?

Very simply, because as Dilip Rao, Venture Financier and Professor at Florida International University, writes in *Forbes*, "your reality will differ from your business plan" whether it is the financial assumptions you make, the sales expectations you have or the environment you operate in. Start-ups that consider alternatives and have fallback strategies in place tend to navigate these unexpected hurdles better than those that have a set tunnel vision.

This does not mean that they waver from their objective, but just reroute every once in a while to get there, keeping practical rather than ideological considerations in mind.

3. Keep the Customer at the Core

As start-ups struggle with a grand overload of teething issues while growing their company, from getting the product/service fit right to marketing, hiring and fundraising, they often lose focus of the most important cog in the wheel—the customer.

But organizations that grow beyond prototype and attain a certain size emphasize on building a customer-focused culture right from the very beginning. They never lose focus of who their beneficiary or customer is and what works in their best interest. While making product and delivery decisions, they take a holistic view of customer needs, get users to participate in delivery, take feedback and incorporate it in the development of their product/service.

This requires filtering feedback loops through the entire organization, and not merely at the top management level. This means empowering employees at the frontier who interact with customers regularly to identify and solve problems rather than using a top-down approach to customer service.

4. Be Conscious of Capital

Organizations that scale innovations successfully build strong capital controls. They are both cost-effective and cost-efficient in their delivery. They use unorthodox methods of fundraising and develop innovative techniques to conserve cash, such as by trying to save on basic start-up costs, standardization of delivery, use of frontier technologies and generation of ancillary revenue that can feed into their core operations and so on and so forth.

Frugality, or the ability to do more from less is a significant virtue. Resources are scarce and being cost-conscious can both make your capital last longer, and give you a significant market advantage which can aid the process of scaling. What it can also do is catalyze radical innovation, says Navi Radjou, a Silicon Valley-based strategy consultant and frugal innovation scholar. According to him "even more than a strategy, frugal innovation is a whole new mindset, a flexible approach that perceives resource constraints not as a debilitating challenge but as a growth opportunity."

In an entrepreneurial culture that is premised upon the erroneous idea that all it takes for a company to succeed is the cushion of funding, approaching growth in a capital-conscious way can be a breakthrough, especially given the limited access Indian entrepreneurs have to capital in comparison to their western counterparts.

5. Hire for Passion, Not Pedigree

It is virtually impossible to bring an idea to scale without the right team in place. Employees are the lifeblood of any company. But getting a great set of people to work for a start-up can be tremendously difficult given its unique constraints—unproven mettle, long hours, limited resources, lack of structure and an uncertain future.

Hiring talent for their passion and belief in the mission of the start-up rather than their pedigree (academic performance, educational qualifications and experience) is thus an absolute necessity in order to scale. Think about it—can your early hires survive the notoriously long hours, salary delays and dramatic pivots/failures that come without prior warning if they are not really passionate about their jobs?

Hire those who believe in the vision and are willing to go the extra mile even if they are not the most qualified for the job. This is vital because skills are transferable, right attitude is not.

6. Build a Culture of Innovation

Innovation is a driving force for profitability and growth. It enhances an organization's competitiveness, and is a key contributor to higher productivity, better business processes and long-term scalability in a fast-changing operating environment that is being rapidly disrupted by new technologies.

But for innovation to thrive at an organizational level, it is crucial that its spirit is not restricted to the leadership, but permeates down to the entire organization so that it creates the hunger to innovate among the ranks. This is accomplished by seeding innovation into the DNA at inception and consciously choosing to build an environment that fosters it across the board.

Some of the ways in which organizations with innovation at their core build a solid culture at an organizational level are:

1. They allow their teams the space and freedom to think and experiment.

2. They build resilience towards failure so that teams are encouraged to take calculated risks.

3. They allow for a cross-pollination of ideas across organizational boundaries and teams.

4. They do everything they can to have an open-door culture that busts hierarchy. Fences and barricades are a big drag on creativity and morale.

5. They encourage diversity of ideas, opinions, talents and temperaments. Research after research has provided evidence of the positive correlation between diversity and improved market outcomes. Monotone organizations encourage insularity, which is never good for business.

7. Constantly Expand Upon Your Vision

If the only constant is change, can a vision crafted in the past remain static for the present?

Companies that gather scale usually make incremental additions/changes to the vision they start off with. They continuously evaluate ways to get bigger and better. Doing things the way they were done in the past does not work and they recognize that. As a result, they do not stagnate upon a vision statement, but reimagine newer possibilities as they inch closer to their initial targets.

One way in which they do this is by constantly keeping an eye on the future and dedicating a part of their resources to planning for the next phase of growth. This may include penetrating newer markets, related diversification of products or services, technological intervention to remain future-ready or even expansion beyond the realms of the company.

Choosing the Trailblazers

Organizations featured in this book have followed all or most of the above tenets. They have succeeded emphatically in taking their innovations not only to an essential scale at the organizational level, but also carved a distinct niche for themselves as market leaders in their chosen areas of operation. While these seven sutras have been big contributing factors to their growth, it is important to bear in mind that they are not a secret one-size-fits-all formula to success.

Elements that are deeply idiosyncratic or unique to each company or sector have played a critical role over and above the essential tenets in determining their success.

For instance, affiliations with non-governmental organizations (NGOs) committed to the same goal have been vital for social impact organizations featured in the book, to spread their impact far and wide quickly. As has been the adoption of the for-profit social enterprise model, a scalable impact model of the future that is self-sustaining, and does not rely on grants and donations.

For organizations across almost all other domains, technology has proved to be a massive catalyst for scaling and leapfrogging their way to growth. Automating business activities and using the power of data and the internet of things (IoT) to connect disaggregated systems on a single unified platform has proved to be the only way to address the complexities that have arisen out of hectic growth and organizations that have embraced these technologies as central to their DNA have triumphed.

Further, process-driven innovations such as unconventional routes to fundraising, and standardized, modular approaches to product development have aided growth in other specific contexts.

A common theme that runs through the scale-up journeys of all the eight organizations featured in the book is the big, bold and ambitious nature of their ideas or innovations, some of which have been global firsts and game changers.

Goonj is an incredible organization that has created a parallel cashless economy, using old clothes as currency for development across large sections of India.

Forus Health has devised an actionable, low-cost solution to prevent avoidable blindness, saving millions of people from being robbed off their vision.

Tonbo Imaging has developed game-changing 'nature-inspired' imaging technology for armed forces across the globe, helping countries fortify their defense systems.

The Better India is a digital purveyor of all the good there is in the world, amplifying the impact of heroes, reformers and trailblazers, and inspiring positive action.

Agastya International Foundation has made it a mission to ignite India's young minds from the bottom up, replacing rote learning with real-life experiential pedagogy to unleash creativity among the poorest of students in the country.

ISRO, India's space research organization, has proved through missions such as the 'Mangalyaan' how galaxies can be traversed on a budget with frugal engineering.

Rivigo has shown how logistics can be hyper tech-enabled and humane at the same time, pioneering a global first relay model that is unparalleled in surface transport.

And **St. Judes** has showcased through its pioneering intervention in pediatric cancer care how building an effective transitional ecosystem can significantly impact recovery outcomes for patients.

The transformative potential of these ideas and the lack

of substitutes for them in the market have been strong propellants towards success at scale for these companies.

The book is divided into eight separate chapters, each featuring an organization. Each chapter itself is further divided into two sections:

I. Biography

II. Business Insights

I have approached every organization's business journey as a biographical narrative rather than as a didactic step-by-step recount of the scale-up story. There is a great deal more insight, both business and inspirational, that these organizations offer to a reader than cut-and-dried sutras for scaling. The compelling, inspirational and personal backstories of the people who make these companies add invaluable nuance and color to their scale-up journeys which are best captured in a storytelling format.

At the end of each chapter though is a detailed summary with clear illustrative examples of the organization's individual sutras to creating, sustaining and scaling innovation, and also of those that are strongly aligned with the overarching framework of the seven scale-up sutras laid out here. These insights add contextual business wisdom for those seeking to dissect the journey from an academic prism.

The book is editorially formatted in such a way that it can have a broad-based appeal for everyone including business leaders looking to glean precious entrepreneurial intelligence, budding entrepreneurs as well as students looking for business stories and inspiration. I hope you enjoy reading it.

Nikhil Inamdar

1

Tonbo Imaging

Defying All Odds

At 5.30 am on September 18, 2016, four militants from across the border in Pakistan sprang a nasty surprise on Indian soil, staging a pre-dawn ambush on an army base in Uri, 6 km from the Line of Control (LoC). Seventeen grenades were fired in a matter of just minutes. This was followed by an intense gun battle that lasted a whole six hours. By the end of it, 19 Indian *jawans* were killed and about 30 were injured in what was termed the deadliest attack on Indian security forces in Kashmir in nearly two and a half decades.

How did the terrorists breach the army's three-tier counter infiltration security system? It is a mystery that baffled investigators later assigned to probe the strike. Uri also demonstrated emphatically that defending India's outer military posts, which are increasingly becoming targets for cross-border militants from Pakistan, is a tough job despite its large defense outlays. But most importantly, the attack raised an important existential question—could such a break-in have been avoided entirely had India's military establishments housed more advanced security and surveillance systems?

While the Indian army has a long way to go before it can claim to have comprehensively upgraded security infrastructure around high-impact targets such as Uri, it is likely that terrorists seeking to infiltrate these installations in the future will have to face up to tougher barriers, namely, the technological might of an obscure little start-up that has been working in close conjunction with the forces to fortify these bases.

> How did the terrorists breach the army's three-tier counter infiltration security system? It is a mystery that baffled investigators later assigned to probe the Uri strike.

The start-up in question is Bengaluru-based Tonbo Imaging.

Founded in 2008 by BITS Pilani and Carnegie Mellon University alumnus Arvind Lakshmikumar along with his colleagues, Tonbo Imaging was born following a management buyout of Sarnoff Corporation's India R&D arm where Lakshmikumar worked for three years between 2004 and 2007 upon his return from the US.

Lakshmikumar had acquired experience as a sub-contractor on several highly-classified next-generation military programs with the National Aeronautics and Space Administration (NASA), the Defense Advanced Research Projects Agency (DARPA) as well as global defense corporations such as Boeing, Lockheed Martin and Future Combat Systems. He says that the start-up was conceived as an idea that would marry his education in intelligent imaging systems with rich experience and networks in the defense industry to build sophisticated imaging technology for the forces.

The Dragonfly

The name 'Tonbo' means dragonfly in Japanese, a fascinating insect with 40,000 eyes, each a miniature sensor-processor in itself. The dragonfly senses data from all these eyes and combines it together to process a final high-resolution image. Its compound structure allows it to perform all kinds of amazing maneuvers, giving it clear sight through low light conditions and helping it navigate difficult terrain such as narrow tunnels at lightning speeds.

It is this small and yet complex creature that inspired Lakshmikumar and his team to ask: could nature's sensing and processing capabilities be emulated for imaging systems?

"Nature shows us that multiple eyes are better than one eye. It is why we've all been endowed with two. But the monolithic architecture of our cameras has not changed for nearly 200 years. They are still single aperture systems that limit the depth of what you are allowed to see," explains Lakshmikumar. "At Tonbo Imaging we began a quest to disrupt the fundamental technology in use behind cameras. The question we asked ourselves as we started the company was, could we borrow from biology to build better cameras for the military?"

While incremental improvements had taken place over the years in optics, sensors and image-processing technology used in cameras, they had not really moved the needle much for better navigation in war-like situations where smoke, dust, fog and military camouflage tactics obstructed vision. In order to circumvent these impediments, it was critical to not just make upgrades to existing technology but redefine the way images were captured.

And Tonbo Imaging has done just that.

It manufactures advanced imaging and sensor systems and night vision devices that work in complex environments where navigation is complicated by smoke, fog and other visual and sensory hindrances. Its vast array of devices fitted with intelligent cameras are appended to guns, drones, unmanned aerial vehicles (UAVs), tanks and other armaments used by the military for reconnaissance in modern battles as well as for commercial applications.

But what is so exceptional about this company, apart from the cutting-edge "nature-inspired technology" it deploys in its cameras, which allows army personnel to navigate challenging conditions?

The answer is that it has defied all odds to make a dashing entry into the largely murky, insular world of Indian defense, pushing its way through an opaque ecosystem that is ill-disposed if not openly hostile to start-ups.

Buyout Beginnings

Arvind Lakshmikumar, the founder of Tonbo Imaging, is a strapping man with movie-star good looks. He was a self-confessed problem child which is why his parents sent him off to the Rashtriya Military School in Bengaluru when he was young. It became an early nurturing ground for his interest in guns and armaments. The school was a great equalizer where the sons of both lieutenants and *jawans* studied in the same classroom and got access to the same kinds of facilities. In the seven years that Lakshmikumar spent at the school, he learnt martial arts, shooting, boxing and other basic skills required for entry into the army.

After completing high school, Lakshmikumar applied to the armed forces and also to BITS Pilani, a premier educational institute known for its engineering, science and management programs. He was selected on merit by both but ended up choosing the latter. As glamorous as a life in the army sounded, his parents cautioned him against the hardships of constant movement.

But while Lakshmikumar chose engineering over the military, little did he know at the time that he would stay connected with his roots in the armed forces perhaps even more intimately than before in his avatar as a defense-tech entrepreneur.

After completing his postgraduate degree in engineering, Lakshmikumar went off to the Carnegie Mellon University in the US, enrolling in a doctoral program in robotics and applied imaging systems. It was during these years that he began concurrently working on projects for various arms of the US Department of Defense, benefitting from the strong industry–academia collaborations that universities in the US offered.

His advisor was a well-reputed man with deep inroads into the defense sector and by association Lakshmikumar was exposed to solid networks, getting a chance to work on highly technical classified programs and earning fellowships from prestigious organizations such as NASA and DARPA. In a matter of five years, Lakshmikumar had a CV decorated with work experience as a sub-contractor on next-generation military programs with the government and some of the biggest global corporations such as Boeing, Lockheed Martin and Future Combat Systems.

But in 2004, he decided to come back to India. His parents were getting old and both he and his wife were keen to return home. Luckily, around this time, Sarnoff Corporation, formerly the Radio Corporation of America, was exploring the idea of setting up an R&D center in Bengaluru. They had cutting-edge research facilities in Princeton and California with 600 PhDs working on core technology products. With his established domain expertise in applied imaging technologies, computer vision robotics and intelligent systems, Lakshmikumar was asked if he would like to head technology and operations for their India function.

It was a sweet coincidence and Lakshmikumar eagerly grabbed the opportunity. The decision would eventually become key in shaping his entrepreneurial destiny.

Sarnoff's intention in India was to commercialize fundamental technologies in computer vision for the automobile industry. But their first few years were spent working on all kinds of random research projects in areas as diverse as space technology, cameras and even predictive analysis of pornographic content for platforms like YouTube. Building and commercializing products needed substantial investment and a commercial bent of mind. But Sarnoff, being a heavily research-oriented firm dependent on grants, was reluctant to risk putting its own capital into a business.

By 2007, Lakshmikumar was keen to step out of the R&D mold and build something that had a real-world application. He made an audacious move, asking Sarnoff to let him do a management buyout of its India R&D center and restructure it into a business start-up with a go-to-market approach.

Sarnoff agreed to the proposal, giving Lakshmikumar everything except access to its IP-protected products. This included its India assets and a set of top-notch hires.

This was how Tonbo Imaging was born.

Starting Over

Acquiring Sarnoff's operations gave Lakshmikumar instant access to the brightest pool of talent, a crucial requirement for a deep technology start-up. But the company was saddled with a large number of unnecessary hires. His first task over six–eight months after the buyout was to get rid of them, letting the start-up bleed till they all found new jobs. By the end of it, he retained only a core team of 5–6 people.

This motley group included all the men and women who continue to steer the Tonbo ship even today: Ankit Kumar, CTO; Sudeep George, vice president, Engineering; Cecelia D'Souza, CFO; Sumeet Suri, global head of Business Development and Jagrut Patel, global head of Sales. They decided to join hands as co-founders and had two critical tasks before them.

The first was to quickly sharpen focus and decide what exactly they were going to build. "As a founder I understood perfectly well that I'd have to choose a domain of operations where I had fundamental experience," says Lakshmikumar. "My background was in intelligent imaging systems, and I had worked for the defense industry, with influential friends and networks that I could leverage as potential customers for a future product. It seemed like a natural fit at that point to marry the two, and build imaging systems for the defense industry."

Whether it was UAVs, submarines, tanks or AK-47s, 30 percent to sometimes as much as 300 percent of the cost of these military systems was attached to their cameras and processors. So, it also made perfect business sense to narrow focus further and concentrate on the eye and the brain of defense artillery.

But with nothing in the bank, the other urgent job before the team was to raise money.

Given how tough it is for funding to come by for defense start-ups in India coupled with the fact that Lakshmikumar did not have a concrete product idea yet, this bit was surprisingly easy. He had friends at the Mumbai Angel Network, an early-stage investor group, and he approached them with a pitch that could only have been made by someone who believed in telling it precisely like it is:

> "I said to them, look, there's no innovation happening in public sector defense companies. They don't have the skillset it takes to build intelligent electro-optic imaging products from ground up. As a nation we are greatly dependent on the US, Russia and Israel who aren't selling us new state-of-the-art technology. Beyond India too, the other emerging economies are undertaking massive modernization of their equipment. There's clearly a market out there for such products. I want to build something that taps this market, but have no clue yet what it is going to be. Could you think of me as someone on a mission like Thomas Edison? He wanted to build a more practical lighting system, but had no indication when he set out that it would be an electrical bulb. I too want to build a more sophisticated camera technology for the army, but have no idea what exactly it will be."

The Angels were disarmed. Here was a man with extensive industry experience, asking for money to explore the possibilities of deep innovation in a specific technology domain for the defense industry, without making any tall promises.

They took a leap of faith and wrote him a check for ₹2 crores.

"[Tonbo] had domain expertise and innovation was their strength, but the key was that they were able to articulate their vision about how they would leverage that innovation to build a successful commercial business," says Anand Ladsariya, angel investor and a member of the Mumbai Angels.[1]

The cash coming in set into motion what would become an eight-year-long period of hyper experimentation.

Striding Through

The Indian defense sector relies predominantly on public sector undertakings (PSUs), government-owned research and development agencies and exports from the US, Israel and Russia for its procurement needs. Despite having a large defense budget, incentives for start-ups and small and medium-sized enterprises (SMEs) to build and commercialize defense technology have been negligible thus far with contracts notoriously slow to come by. As a result, the sector has remained an elite playfield of the big boys from India Inc. and their global counterparts with solid influence in the corridors of power. It is a space riddled with cross-border scams and high-level corruption and run by a network of middlemen who are difficult to get past.

But Tonbo Imaging has emerged as one among a very tiny inventory of Indian start-ups threatening to unseat the monopoly of this established lot. It has done this through a sharply-crafted dual strategy of business process and product innovation, devised over these eight years of experimentation. In this period, it modeled itself as an asset-light company that followed the Apple Inc. model, outsourcing non-critical processes and focusing only on building strong intellectual property to counter the might of vertically-integrated legacy players such as Lockheed Martin, Raytheon, Dassault Systèmes, Boeing and others.

> After clocking in virtually zero revenue through the first four years of its existence when it concentrated on building technology, the start-up has seen a spectacular scale-up in operations in the past four years.

Within just a decade of its founding, the company has been able to serve not just its home base, but the globe's military needs. It counts among its clients, 25 marquee names across 25 geographies such as NASA, the US Navy Sea, Air and Land Teams (SEALs), the Peruvian army, the Border Security Force (BSF), the Central Reserve Police Force (CRPF), the Defence Research and Development Organization (DRDO), the National Security Guard (NSG), the Northern Command of the Army and DARPA, the technology branch of the US Department of Defense, to name just a few. It has also conducted important pilots with Tesla and Uber, expanding the scope of its products' applications to civilian realms such as vehicle safety and autonomous operations.

After clocking in virtually zero revenue through the first four years of its existence when it concentrated on building technology, the start-up has seen a spectacular scale up in operations in the past four years. Growing at 80–100 percent per annum, its revenues have crossed the $200 million mark, and it has raised over $30 million through two rounds of funding from blue-chip investors such as Artiman Ventures, WRV Capital, Qualcomm Ventures and Edelweiss Private Equity and Capital. It is now on the cusp of raising another $250 million to foray into bigger domains.

With a headcount that has jumped from 5 to 150, Tonbo Imaging is rapidly expanding its global footprint as well with offices in Lithuania, Singapore, the US and Bengaluru. It has filed five patents and inked massive $100 plus million deals, such as the one with the Peruvian army to manufacture 'night vision sights' for rifles, which has earned it the coveted badge of India's largest exporter of defense technology.

So how did this fledgling start-up from India's software capital make inroads so quickly into global defense corridors? What did it take for an entity with barely any capital, zero political influence or fancy global tie-ups to make such breakthroughs and set itself up on the path to potentially exponential scale?

The Tech Advantage

From a product standpoint, what Tonbo has built is technologically path-breaking.

While traditional camera systems rely on a single aperture principle with the burden of image formation placed excessively on the optics, Tonbo's intelligent imaging technology uses both the eye and the brain to process a better picture, what the company calls "a multi-sensor fusion imaging technology that can simultaneously see both heat (infrared spectrum) and light (visible spectrum) and fuse them into one image."

It is a highly technical innovation that uses sophisticated electronics and computational techniques. In layman terms, it is essentially an infrared camera technology that allows human beings, who can see only in the visible spectrum, to do high-end image processing through cameras that can capture low-light conditions and sense, understand and control complex environments during day and night. This was precisely what the military market needed since soldiers operated in dusty, low-visibility environments in which traditional camera technology could not adequately do the job.

"Like the dragon fly's eye, our technology enables the use of many apertures and so instead of needing more light, we end up having more images. This has allowed us to make lighter imaging devices at much lower costs than others, that are also far more sophisticated in their capacity to capture better photos," explains Lakshmikumar, adding that Tonbo is only one of two companies in the world to have developed this technology.[2]

Not only has this dramatically enhanced front-end optics for the defense forces, it is also significantly better than the systems that were in use in terms of size, cost and power, disrupting electro-optics systems in use in the global military market.

Underpinned by this technology, the company has since 2014 gone on to build a wide suite of close to 30 night vision, thermal imaging and long-range surveillance products. They are all hinged upon the same principle, but with applications across not just defense but also civilian areas such as automotive, security and industrial surveillance.

"It's essentially the same camera system, but with different manifestations across different sectors and form factors such as guns, missiles or tanks," explains Lakshmikumar. "We built multiple products—from ultra-light weight sensors to rugged stabilized multi-function electro-optics—but they basically all used our thermal and fused imaging technology. The hardware changes form, but the software remains the same."

Breaking Entry Barriers

But while a transformative imaging product grounded in deep technology is an important USP for a defense start-up, it is by no means a guarantee for success in a procurement ecosystem where the barriers to entry are formidable and cultural incompatibility between vendor and customer very high.

"A lot of start-ups fail when they make the transition from concept to commercialization, but Tonbo had it all figured out," says Anand Ladsariya of the Mumbai Angels.[3]

So how did Lakshmikumar do it? What smarts did he use to crack through the opaque market? And what business process innovation did he bring in to compete with asset-heavy, vertically-integrated competitors in order to get his product to market with speed, scale and efficiency?

For centuries, technology was born on the battlefield. From air travel to nylon synthetics and penicillin to microwave ovens, historically, it is from the military that we have seen some of the most prevalent technologies trickle down into the commercial market.

In the last 15–20 years however, the pace of technological advancement in the consumer electronics market has vastly outdone the defense sector, creating a ready ecosystem of products or components for defense start-ups to tap into.

"If you look at defense products, they are no different from a mobile phone from an architectural standpoint. In fact, the electronics that goes into your smartphone is often more sophisticated than what goes into a predator drone.

So, we thought, why not reverse the course of history and leverage technological advancements already made in the commercial market to build for the defense industry?" says Lakshmikumar.

This inverted approach would serve two purposes. By riding the consumer electronics wave, Tonbo would not need to invest heavily into big manufacturing facilities unlike its traditional competitors like Raytheon or BAE who had to also make their own electronic, processing and optical components. It could structure itself as an asset-light technological platform, focusing on its core competency of building night vision and thermal imaging technology, and simply outsource the non-critical parts of the manufacturing process to a ready ecosystem of licensed contractors.

"Every asset-heavy industry was being disrupted by tech platforms—Uber in mobility, Apple in manufacturing or Airbnb in hospitality. We too decided we would own only the brand, the customer and the supply chain, and not have an assembly line at all," says Lakshmikumar. "There were so many original equipment manufacturers (OEMs) across the world already making chips, sensors, lenses, printed circuit boards and everything else that went into our products for smartphone companies. It would take us a long time and a lot of capital to replicate what they did, so we decided to focus only on building core intellectual property and nothing else. Our competitors didn't have this advantage when they started out because this ecosystem was absent."

Among the first companies Lakshmikumar approached with a request to license a component was Qualcomm, the American semiconductor and telecommunications equipment behemoth whose chips were used in millions of mobile handsets sold by manufacturers such as Sony,

Samsung and Motorola Mobility. His requirement was for a few hundred chipsets, but Qualcomm told him they sold only in the millions and only to cell phone manufacturers.

Not deterred, Lakshmikumar directly contacted Paul Jacobs, the company's then chairman, and sought a meeting. Jacobs was an extremely accessible man and agreed to give his ear to the persistent entrepreneur from Bengaluru. Lakshmikumar told him that while it was not a volumes game, if he succeeded in what he was setting out to do, they were looking at a potential transformation in camera technology for military applications. All they needed was for Qualcomm to license their chipsets with the internals cleaned up so that he could put his own software in.

The market was overrun with brokers and resellers, not original manufacturers. They did not care for specs and usually procured the cheapest equipment in order to successfully participate in the bid.

The proposal got Jacobs excited and soon enough Tonbo Imaging became the first licensee for Qualcomm's chipsets used for non-mobile applications. Lakshmikumar forged other similar partnerships with OEMs across the world for sensors, optics and lenses.

Tonbo would design the camera systems, changing the form factor of its product depending on use and application, and get it manufactured from someone. It would prove to become a hugely successful strategy, giving the company the ability to offer its clients a cost advantage of as much as 50 percent in comparison to other defense players, a critical plus point in the price-sensitive Indian market where the most significant customer was the Indian army.

"Defense in India is all about being L1," says Lakshmikumar, using a bidding terminology that denotes the lowest offer in a tender. The reason Tonbo could offer a cost advantage, deliver a substantially better product and still be the lowest bidder (L1) was because it did not have fixed operating costs on things like labor and idle factories that asset-heavy companies had to factor in. Also, the market was overrun with brokers and resellers, not original manufacturers. They did not care for specs and usually procured the cheapest equipment in order to successfully participate in the bid and emerge L1. Then, each of them in the chain added a substantial markup margin to the equipment, taking the price of something that cost ₹20 to ₹100 by the time it was tendered.

Tonbo could make it with far better specs for ₹30 and sell it for ₹50 and still make a substantial margin because it cut out the middlemen.

"My sales pitch to my Indian customers was, if you ask me for a Maruti, I'll give you an Audi, but still be L1 or the lowest bidder," says Lakshmikumar.

Despite this cost advantage, it would take Tonbo Imaging sales to four big global clients before the Indian army would consider onboarding them as a vendor. Such was the aversion to entertain start-ups that Lakshmikumar's attempts to enter the fray were repeatedly scuttled. Then one day, a few army personnel at a global trade show spotted their cutting-edge night vision equipment in use at the US Special Operations Command and BAE Systems booths. That, at last, was sufficient validation.

In hindsight, this hidebound attitude of the Indian army worked in Tonbo Imaging's favor. It urged Lakshmikumar to set his sights on becoming a global player rather than remain an India-centric company. Today, only 30–35 percent of his revenue comes from the army. The rest of it is from global clients in the US, South East Asia, Middle East, Africa and South America.

Defying Funding Hurdles

For Lakshmikumar, the other great challenge to steering such fundamental innovation besides breaking entry barriers and a hostile attitude from Indian customers was raising funds after the first angel round.

In countries like the US, funding for such risky, long-gestation deep technology ideas comes from two generous sources—Silicon Valley venture capitalists, and grants from the US Department of Defense. In India, both these options were closed to him.

"The Indian government doesn't give start-ups any sizable grants, and if you go to traditional VCs in India to raise money for a hardcore technology product, they will tell you in all likelihood that it is not of interest to them," says Lakshmikumar. Most venture capitals (VCs) in India, he says, asked for quick returns. "Their attention span was only about three–five years. They liked to invest in momentum stocks, or sectors that were the flavor of the day, such as e-commerce, retail or mobile. But if you told them you were a company developing imaging technology and sensors they were confounded. They were comfortable investing in me-too companies whose business models had succeeded elsewhere, but not at ease with those that were trying to innovate fundamentally."[4]

By 2010, Lakshmikumar had exhausted the angel money he had raised from Mumbai Angels. And over 15 months, between 2010 and 2012, Lakshmikumar knocked on all possible doors for help. He approached most of the big corporate houses which had a presence in the defense sector through his network of contacts.

But all attempts to explain his ideas were stonewalled by an approach that suggested that they were only interested in a quick business opportunity, not in developing fundamental technology. They wanted to enter the sphere through established partnerships, with global companies that knew how to navigate the complex procurement system and win big contracts rather than build a ground-up cutting-edge defense technology company.

While at the time, this was a cause for immense frustration for Lakshmikumar, in retrospect he thanks his lucky stars for not partnering with the big behemoths.

"Some of them messed up badly with their investments in other defense start-ups," says Lakshmikumar. "They didn't really understand how the space operated, and killed some very good entrepreneurial ideas by pressuring founders about business plans and quick returns."

Thankfully the solution to Tonbo's financial quandaries came in the form of an early-stage sector agnostic venture fund called Artiman Ventures, a Silicon Valley-based VC firm started by a team of six former entrepreneurs who in their own words brought "empathy, curiosity, passion, experience and (occasionally) patience to the table". They invested in "entrepreneurs building white space companies" that had the "potential to create or disrupt multi-billion markets".

Tonbo fit the bill perfectly.

Within six weeks of Lakshmikumar's approaching Artiman Ventures, they decided to put in money purely on the basis of the merit of his idea. Such was their commitment that they even loaned him a top-up amount for operational expenses without the requisite paperwork in place a year after Series-A.

"They didn't even ask me what my previous year's revenues were," says Lakshmikumar who finally raised over \$6 million from the Silicon Valley-based investors by the end of 2012, giving Mumbai Angels an exit from their investment in the angel round with three times the returns.

Empowering Deep Innovation

While the padding of start-up capital is a crucial factor for success for any entrepreneurial venture, for a deep technology company like Tonbo, achieving what it did in such a short span also required leveraging multiple structural and organizational strategies that focused on stimulating and rewarding innovative behavior. This in essence entailed sharp practices on hiring, people management and performance incentives.

Entrepreneurs can be possessive people and micro-managing every task can often become a "start-up sickness" that obstructs their broader vision.[5] Lakshmikumar did not let himself be afflicted by this shortcoming and dedicated his efforts to hiring the best people for the job and giving them the ultimate freedom to explore a problem.

Very early on, Tonbo decided to tap into the global talent pool and hire the smartest guys from across the world. While Indian universities are great at churning out software engineers and programmers who build applications for the information technology (IT) industry, there is a severe shortage of people with an education in electronics, the sciences and physics who understand how to build fundamental systems. For Tonbo, speed was of the essence in order to take a deep technology product from concept to commercialization before it became obsolete, and hiring inexperienced graduates or even experienced hands from public sector competitors would have meant wasting long periods of time on training them.

"As CEO I made a conscientious decision to invest on a very smart team and delegate work to them instead of doing everything myself. I did not participate in the product development process. My job till date is to raise the money, give my team the constraints within which they have to build, such as the wattage, specs or budgets, and leave them to execute it, so that I can focus on business development, investor relations and other commercial responsibilities

> For Tonbo, speed was of the essence in order to take a deep technology product from concept to commercialization before it became obsolete.

concurrently," says Lakshmikumar, who after his experience with Sarnoff was mindful not to isolate himself in pure play R&D and risk ignoring the business side of things.

Apart from computer vision in which he had domain expertise, he hired top-notch scientists in all other fields and allowed them the breathing space to do their job. "We let people fail and make mistakes. We told them to move ahead and learn from their failures rather than penalize them for it. It was a great motivator to do better," says Lakshmikumar.

This hands-off approach also allowed Tonbo Imaging to staff its functions with a large disaggregated global workforce that is today building the most sophisticated electro-optic systems without handholding. The company remained geography agnostic, and hired from Germany, Ukraine, Estonia, Poland, Singapore and Florida. Its head of mechanical engineering for instance, a 65-year-old gentleman with 30 years' experience, sits in Greece and controls a ten-member team sitting in India.

In fact, it is this hunt for the best talent that informed Tonbo's decision to set up an R&D center in Lithuania focusing on lasers and photonics. The small Baltic nation which lies at the intersection of Western Europe and Russia provides the company European infrastructure and Soviet-era know-how at a price that is lower than what he would have spent on hiring less capable talent in India.

In order to foster the spirit of innovation in each and every employee, Tonbo also almost entirely collapsed organizational hierarchy, dispensing with the practice of appointing managers. So today, when a group is assigned a project, all its members are held equally responsible for the outcome. They are closely observed over a period of six–eight months and in Lakshmikumar's experience a natural leader generally emerges in this period and takes charge of the cluster. It is only then that he or she is officially designated to lead for a period of a year or so before being asked to move to another team so that someone else has a shot.

"Just like nature decides that the alpha lion is the king of the jungle, we too depend on a leader's natural instinct to appear rather than pre-assigning them a designation," says Lakshmikumar, giving an example of how the group's leadership philosophies are consistently borrowed from nature. He gives the example of the man who heads Tonbo's Practical Systems Group. A diploma holder who earned far lesser than his peers, he is now heading a team of 30 people far more educated or experienced than him.

"For three years he demonstrated a natural ability to lead and he moved up the ranks organically," he says.

Retaining such talent required paying globally competitive market salaries and offering attractive stock options. Lakshmikumar was mindful of that right from the beginning. So Tonbo offers twice and sometimes up to three times the remuneration given by PSU competitors like DRDO or Bharat Electronics Ltd., subverting a common practice among start-ups of paying recruits a pittance.

When he raised Series-A funding from Artiman Ventures, Lakshmikumar also split his shares in a 60:40 ratio, where 40 percent of the company was owned by him and the remainder by employees, an almost unheard-of precedent in the start-up world where founders desperately hankered for majority control. "I don't believe in promoter-run companies where a single person owns the majority of the shares. A modern business needs to be completely democratic and create shared value for employees especially if they've shared the risk with you. It is the only way to retain good people," says Lakshmikumar.

It is a strategy that has paid him rich dividends in the long run, keeping the company's attrition rate strictly in check.

The Big Gameplan

Today, Tonbo Imaging has achieved in a decade what major defense electronics companies such as Thales Group or SAGEM did in a century.

"We've made our money stretch a lot," says Lakshmikumar. "We've been able to do in $30 million of investment what these companies would have spent half a billion dollars doing. Our product portfolio of 30 different products is today larger than the combined product portfolio of

SAGEM, Thales or Elbit Systems. They've spent 20–30 times we have and over a longer period to get to where we got in $30 million. We haven't needed to spend as much capital because we outsourced manufacturing to contractors."

It is a stupendous achievement, but after ten years of making cutting-edge electro-optic systems for the defense sector, Lakshmikumar has bigger dreams.

Tonbo Imaging currently sells its weapon sights to two kinds of customers—practical systems manufacturers such as rifle companies who can directly mount its sights (or camera technology) on their devices without any system integration, and platform manufacturers who make larger artillery such as battle tank platforms, missiles, fighter jets, etc., where its payload has to be integrated. This is the market where big-ticket procurements for hundreds of millions of dollars' worth of armaments happens, and is fundamental to building scale.

But when armies buy big battle tanks or aerial systems, they prefer to procure the sights from the same vendor in an integrated package. In order to circumvent its lack of presence in platform manufacturing—building structures or systems on which a weapon can be mounted—Tonbo has currently inked unique partnerships with blue-chip companies such as Dassault Rafale and Airbus to jointly pitch to military clients. Through these partnerships the former integrates its sights on to the latter's platforms but without the restrictions on technology transfer imposed by manufacturers in Israel, Russia or Europe.

A great example of this partnership model was seen in the $100 million contract Tonbo bagged to supply night vision sights to UWS which won a bid from the Peruvian army or Fábrica de Armas Municiones del Ejército (FAME) to assemble and jointly manufacture 300,000 rifles. Tonbo's sights, named after Arjuna, the warrior prince from the *Mahabharata* known for his archery skills, trumped top-notch defense players such as BAE Systems Plc, L-3 Communications Holdings Inc. and FLIR Systems Inc. to bag the contract, no mean achievement given that India does not exactly have a global reputation for defense technology exports.

It was the collaboration with a global player like UWS as well as the transfer of technology to Peru at no additional cost, whereby local technicians there would be trained to assemble and make modern rifles and weapon sights, that sealed the deal. It enticed the government because it was not merely a transactional contract. It was a partnership that created local jobs as well.

While this strategy has been successful thus far in helping the company scale up and win large contracts, Lakshmikumar no longer wants to be co-dependent on platform manufacturers in order to participate in bids. This is why he has now set his eyes on acquisitions.

"I want to now buy platform companies in Eastern Europe who make anti-tank guided missiles, remote controlled weapon systems, 30 mm guns, etc. Over the next five years we want to transition from being just a camera supplier to a defense sub-systems supplier that also owns some of the platforms," says Lakshmikumar. This, he believes, will help the company offer its clients a completely integrated package. "They already know us as an electro-optic systems company, and we will leverage our inroads with these clients to offer them fully-integrated platforms," he adds.

Tonbo wants to continue to remain an asset-light player though. So, the vision is not to manufacture heavy platforms such as aircrafts or tanks but only smaller practical systems such as guns and rifles. "We want to do this without being too capital-intensive or through full vertical integration," says Lakshmikumar who needs about \$25–30 million to explore inorganic growth opportunities in Eastern Europe and buy companies in this space.

He is already in the market talking to private equity players and sovereign wealth funds to raise \$250 million over the next two years. He wants to give his current investors an exit, expand through the acquisition route in the platform space and also invest in the company's growing footprint in the autonomous vehicles sector. In Lithuania, Tonbo has already spent about \$10 million in developing a smart transport system technology that will increase the reliability of autonomous vehicles and reduce their price.

While defense will remain the core of its operations, "we want to be anywhere where you need to sense, navigate or understand the environment," says Lakshmikumar. "We want to be the next BAE Systems or Raytheon. They started with an expertise and built several things around it."

Sutras to Creating, Sustaining and Scaling Innovation:
Business Insights from Tonbo Imaging's Journey

Tonbo Imaging is a classic new-age asset-light business that has built its model around optimizing existing ecosystems to create a high-value technology platform. It is a deep technology product company that derives its worth not from the ownership of physical but intellectual assets, and this has fundamentally changed the way it does business, the speed at which it can go to the market, the cost benefit it can afford to its customers and the valuation it commands.

It is also a fundamental product disruptor, changing the paradigm for defense imaging technologies with its cutting-edge technical innovation that can now be optimized even in commercial realms.

Its scale-up story is a consequence of several complex, concurrent organizational strategies designed to create an environment under which innovation could thrive. And the company displays full adherence to at least six of our seven essential attributes for product, process or business-model innovation.

Organiza-tion	Gap in the Market, Market in the Gap?	Flexible Approach	Customer Centricity	Capital Con-scious-ness	Hiring – Passion over Pedigree	Culture of Innova-tion	Amplifi-cation of Vision
Tonbo Imaging	✓	✓		✓	✓	✓	✓

Gap in the Market, Market in the Gap: Gaps exist everywhere including in the armed forces. For an entrepreneur, the challenge lies in finding one that he can actually exploit using his particular skill, experience and networks. It is no use spotting a gap, no matter how pertinent, if it is beyond one's capacity to plug.

Arvind Lakshmikumar carefully established his precise problem statement, and ascertained his ability to fill the gap before he decided to enter the fray. He did this by marrying his skill in imaging technologies with his experience in the defense industry and gauged his ability to leverage a network of contacts needed to penetrate a difficult sector. It was only after all the three criteria fell into place that he decided to put his money where his mouth was.

The approach was much the same while creating a market for his product. He knew he needed to focus on three things concurrently in order to succeed in a sector that did not give start-ups a chance:

- A breakthrough product that delivered higher specs than industry peers, but at a lower cost to remain L1 in a price-sensitive market.

- An asset-light, platform-driven business model that would restrict capital spend and improve speed of delivery.

- The global validation of product portfolio through international sales to get footing into the closed Indian defense market.

It was this three-pronged strategy that allowed Tonbo Imaging to create a firm footing for itself in the defense business in a fraction of the time it took its global competitors.

Flexible Approach: When Lakshmikumar started Tonbo Imaging, his motivation was to supply principally to the Indian armed forces. But plotting a course through the complex defense bureaucracy was tough. Bureaucrats made unreasonable demands of Lakshmikumar, such as asking him to put DRDO logos on his products or surrender his IP. He did not sell himself short merely in order to win a contract, but was both patient and flexible enough to pivot.

Since things were not working out in India, he decided to aggressively tap global military programs and reposition the company as an international player that would make products for the world market. Today Tonbo's global revenue is 50 percent and expected to increase significantly going forward.

"A pivot changes any of nine different things in a company's business model: product, customer segment, your distribution channel, revenue model/pricing, resources, activities, costs, partners and customer acquisition," says Geri Stengel, a contributor at *Forbes*.[6]

In Tonbo's case, being open to this pivot changed many of these things, and became key to Lakshmikumar's entrepreneurial success at a global level, which he then used to make an entry into the Indian market.

Capital Consciousness: Lakshmikumar claims to have done in $30 million what took over half a billion dollars in investments for its global peers. He attributes a large part of this ability to "stretch the money" to the company's asset-light, capital-light business model and nominal expenses on marketing, sales or trade shows. Since it integrates its sights on platforms manufactured by bigger, established companies, Tonbo benefits from default publicity through them. The company has also kept its administrative expenses to a minimum, functioning out of a nondescript homestyle headquarters in Bengaluru, and spends a majority of its funds on R&D and talent acquisition, two critical components to providing a defense technology start-up the most bang for its buck.

Hiring – Passion over Pedigree: Despite the highly technical nature of the work it does, the lack of a degree is no bar for entry into Tonbo Imaging. Lakshmikumar himself is a PhD dropout and does not give a great deal of importance to educational qualifications. He has people with just a diploma heading teams with more experienced people in them. But the company's interview process is demanding and geared towards finding out what a candidate can do rather than what they have done in the past. Interviewees are often expected to spend the whole day demonstrating their flare with the hardware in front of them rather than answering theoretical questions.

"We try and assess a potential employee's frame of mind and see whether it gels with our way of working," says Lakshmikumar. "We need people who can work in an unstructured environment and take initiative, rather than be expected to be told what they should be doing." He believes that it is a fair way of filtering out those who do not come with an original bent of mind.

Culture of Innovation: Lakshmikumar has four clearly spelt-out mantras that allow a strong culture of innovation to penetrate down the ranks. These include:

- Creating a flat organization by dispensing with designations such as manager, project lead, etc. At Tonbo when a new hire joins, no matter how senior he might be, he is referred to as 'programming staff'. Leaders at Tonbo are born naturally, their positions are not pre-assigned on the basis of seniority or educational qualifications;

- Sharing the spoils of innovation through a generous policy on stock options and globally competitive salaries;

- Giving staff full freedom to experiment and fail, as long as certain essential norms are not violated;

- Hiring the smartest people even if it means higher HR outlays and managing a disaggregated global workforce.

Amplification of Vision: Tonbo started with a brave mission to revolutionize imaging technology and improve navigation in complex environments by giving defense artillery a better eye and brain. But having conquered that domain, it now wants to own the body as well. No longer content being an electro-optics systems supplier, the company has set its sights on owning platforms.

It could be a move fraught with risk: Tonbo does not have experience running manufacturing companies or dealing with the complexity of an asset-heavy industrial entity. But it may well be a logical move up the value chain. By vertically integrating its operations bit by bit to scale the final frontier, it may become what it wishes to be—the next BAE Systems or Raytheon with a presence that far exceeds the realms of defense.

References

1. "Tonbo Imaging – A Strong Defence," *Outlook Business*, June 2, 2016. https://www.outlookbusiness.com/specials/power-of-i_2016/tonbo-imaging-a-strong-defence-2797

2. "Finally, A Cutting Edge Technology Company From India; In Conversation with Arvind Lakshmikumar, Founder, Tonbo Imaging," *YourStory*, October 30, 2012. https://yourstory.com/2012/10/finally-a-cutting-edge-technology-company-from-india-in-conversation-with-arvind-lakshmikumar-from-tonbo-imaging

3. "Tonbo Imaging – A Strong Defence."

4. "A Cutting Edge Technology Company: In Conversation with Arvind, Founder, Tonbo. https://www.youtube.com/

watch?v=2C2ntkxFllQ

5.   "When Entrepreneurs Micromanage: A Start-up Sickness,"
     Inc., July 3, 2014. https://www.inc.com/john-boitnott/
     when-entrepreneurs-micromanage-a-start-up-sickness.html

6.   "Flexibility And Change Can Be Keys To Entrepreneurial
     Success," *Forbes*, December 27, 2017. https://www.forbes.
     com/sites/geristengel/2017/12/27/flexibility-change-can-
     be-keys-to-entrepreneurial-success/

2

Goonj

Urban Surplus as Currency for Rural Development

The women of Pipronia begin their song en masse, blowing heaps of dust in the air as the children, lolling about outside the primary school, shriek with delight. It is around noon. The glare of the winter sun is blindingly brilliant, but work is on in full swing at this remote hamlet situated on a stubborn, rocky patch of land. Eighty five families from the village have gathered to make an ascending road that will connect their homes directly to their fields beyond.

Once complete, the dirt track will be an asset for this small community in Uttar Pradesh's Bundelkhand region. This land's past glory is marred by poverty in the present day. The newly-paved road will enable tractors to arrive at the farms directly thus saving the villagers a grueling slog every day. In return for their hard work, each person will receive clothes, shoes, utensils and other essential items of daily use instead of hard cash.

These aren't people who earn wages under the Mahatma Gandhi National Rural Employment Guarantee Act

(MGNREGA) or any of the other state and central social security programs that attempt, with questionable efficacy, to provide employment and livelihood to rural laborers in the country's poorest regions. What they are part of is a full-size people's movement for development, underway across the length and breadth of India, accepting not CASH but TRASH in return for their toil.

They are part of Goonj, an organization that has over the 20 years of its existence transformed the very concept of giving (and receiving) in India. It has connected the urban surplus of material with a rural deficit for the same and then used it as legitimate currency for developmental work in the remotest regions of the country.

Goonj accomplishes this through a well-structured, systematic, process-driven supply chain. Through collection drives across cities, it gathers old clothing, footwear, stationery, books and anything else that people may want to give away. These items are then given a new lease of life through careful sorting and reprocessing at large centers across the country where they are bundled into 15–20 kilos of gunny sacks called 'family kits', customized closely to the needs of the recipient families. They are then distributed to small villages like Pipronia.

But not for free!

Goonj collaborates with rural village communities across India, nudging them to identify their own neglected community and infrastructural needs and solve them with their own efforts, resources and wisdom. It gets villagers to take up activities such as repairing roads and bridges, digging wells, cleaning ponds, reviving basic infrastructure and improving living standards in the villages. In exchange for their participation and as a reward for their efforts, villagers are given the kits through its flagship 'Cloth for Work' program.

The outcomes of its work are visible in the curbed migration, improved sanitation and better-preserved local ecologies.

In the Sundarbans for instance, in return for its rehabilitation efforts and clothing kits, Goonj got local communities to plant mangrove saplings across a length of the shoreline that was affected by Cyclone Aila. Today, these saplings have blossomed into full-grown mangroves and are acting as a shield against other calamities in this disaster-prone region.

In Champaran, Bihar, cursed by poverty and alcohol abuse, it was intervention by Goonj that finally proved to be the panacea. A chance to learn the art of quilt-making (in return for a village clean-up drive) made the women of the Tharu Tola village give up liquor production, a profession that had sustained this forest populace for decades.

More recently, in Orissa, Goonj got women self-help groups in the village of Malabiharpur to clean the only freshwater lake in the state, thereby reviving tourism in the region and providing the locals with a much-needed alternate source of income. And of course a 'Cloth for Work' kit.

There are many such stories and what becomes evident across the narratives is the remarkable success with which Goonj has mobilized people to take collective responsibility for their own problems through a participatory form of self-governance. It has put the act of decision-making back in the people's own hands and has become a seminal drive that uses cloth—not as charity, but as currency—to create a parallel cashless economy, thereby changing mindsets and empowering communities in regions where state or corporate help does not reach.

Today, Goonj is recognized as an organization that has

truly redefined the idea of charity by shifting the focus of giving from "the donor's pride, to the receiver's dignity", turning the age-old conception on its head.

The Bridgemaker

Founded in 1999 by Delhi-based communications professional Anshu Gupta, Goonj was born out of its founder's desire to position the right to clothing as a neglected developmental goal.

In 1991, Uttarakhand was devastated by an earthquake. Anshu who was in college at the time went on a photography trip to the region and saw an old man, wrapped in a tattered gunny sack, beseeching relief workers for a blanket. The man didn't ask for food, water or medicine. All he wanted was something to protect himself with from the biting cold.

It was then that Anshu realized that for the poor, the very phenomenon of winter, as much as any other natural calamity, spelt disaster.

Later that year, while roaming outside the Lok Nayak Jai Prakash Narayan (LNJP) hospital in Old Delhi, a sign on a rickshaw caught his eye. It said *"Lawaris Lash Uthane Wala"* or "Lifter of Unclaimed Dead Bodies". Intrigued, Anshu followed the rickshaw owner who he later discovered was called Habib on his rounds. He noticed that the old man would pick up abandoned bodies and carry them to the crematorium for ₹20 and two meters of white cloth per body. In the summers, Habib collected around four-five bodies every day. In the winters, that number would swell to between 10 and 20. In fact, there were so many that he couldn't handle the load.

Habib's daughter Bano made an even more startling

revelation. "I hug the dead body and sleep when I feel cold," she said. "It doesn't trouble me, twist or turn."

The incident shook Anshu deeply. It made him realize that it wasn't just the cold but also the lack of clothing that killed people in this country.

But clothing was never a priority for non-profit agencies or the government. It was discussed only in the context of disaster relief. Anshu's interactions with people like Habib showed him that this was a big developmental gap that needed to be addressed. His suspicions were confirmed by data which revealed that people in rural and even urban slum communities couldn't afford to purchase new clothes for years.

"We spoke about *roti, kapda, makan* (food, clothing, shelter) as three basic needs of humanity. In the list of development issues spoken about globally, everything from domestic abuse to global warming was included, but the basic need for clothing was not paid enough attention to. But looking at the ground realities I knew that cloth had to be brought to the forefront of the development debate," says Anshu.

And so, after toying with the idea for a few years, Anshu left his job as a corporate communications professional at Escorts to start Goonj with a mission to bring about the change he desired, initially with 67 pieces of clothing from his and his wife Meenakshi's closet as capital.

Today, 20 years later, Goonj deals with over 4,000 tons of used material every year. This includes things urban India discards, like clothes, school material, shoes, utensils, office equipment, doors and windows. It is present in 24 states, through a network of 250 partner groups which include grassroots organizations, NGOs, social activists, panchayats, the Indian army and its own implementation teams which together with rural communities trigger nearly 4,000 grassroots rural development activities every year under the 'Cloth for Work' initiative. With nearly 1,000 employees, Goonj has also become one of the biggest disaster relief and rehabilitation agencies, and stands as a node at the thorny intersections of our development agenda. It has located itself between urban surplus and rural deficit, disaster mitigation and relief provision, and bridges difficult divides through sustained innovation, thereby gaining a size that very few social organizations have managed.

The Goonj Doctrine

What has enabled Goonj's staggering growth? What did it do differently to keep itself from becoming just another charity organization? There are after all many nonprofits out there that start off with grand intentions but fail to expand beyond a hyper local milieu. What did Goonj do that catapulted it into a new stratosphere altogether?

Anshu and Meenakshi started with no money, contacts or influence in the right places. In the very year in which they began, a terrible cyclone hit Odisha, and they managed to mobilize supplies from their friends and relatives to send as relief material. But in order to gather critical scale, more people beyond their immediate circle needed to know about the work. This was a time when social media had not yet gained ground and reaching out to people about their idea was a challenge.

To circumvent the problem, the couple set up a small arts and crafts stall in Dilli Haat, Delhi where Anshu would sell bamboo clocks. Here, they kept fliers detailing Goonj's activities and asked customers to leave messages on their answering machine if they were keen to donate old clothes. That did the job. They would get 10–15 messages every day from people who were eager to discard material. So even though the clocks sold out in two days, the couple kept the stall for a few more weeks and frantically made new clocks in a small workshop at the rear so that they could continue interacting with more people to spread the word about Goonj.

> People are generally reluctant to part with their money and find it difficult to trust others with it. Conversely, they are only too happy to discard what they no longer use for a good cause.

People took to their earnest, straightforward approach. That they weren't asking for money perhaps appealed to many and the effort gathered considerable traction through word-of-mouth recommendations. In a matter of a few months, their home, which had become the de facto Goonj office where donated clothes would come in and be washed overnight by the couple themselves to be distributed later, ran out of space and they had to rent another small space to store and process the material.

Very early into its operations, Anshu had an unusually clear vision about how he wanted to approach the idea of giving. As a conscious strategy he decided that he wouldn't ask people for money, but for what was bothering them and taking up unnecessary space, i.e., their surplus clothes and other household material. Therein lay his first big breakthrough. People are generally reluctant to part with their money and find it difficult to trust others with it. Conversely, they are only too happy to discard what they no longer use for a good cause. It is both a path of least resistance and a positive reinforcement of one's self-image.

Anshu perceptively noticed this problem at the urban end where people bought more and more but did not have a reliable channel to discard the surplus. He built this aspect into the core idea of Goonj, thereby solving a big problem that most social start-ups face in their early stages, i.e., of resources. In Goonj's case, however, the funding came not in the form of cash but quite literally in the form of trash or other people's refuse.

What also helped was the early recognition that the urban discard he collected should be distributed among the needy in rural areas as reward and not charity, in essence giving Goonj the ability to effect change at three levels—addressing their basic material-needs gap, solving their community-developmental needs and helping them acquire a sense of dignity.

This was an idea that came to Anshu and Meenakshi first when they asked slum dwellers residing under a flyover outside their house in Sarita Vihar, Delhi, if they could clean up the area in return for a few old clothes. They readily agreed to the offer and it made the duo realize that for Goonj to sustain and grow, they needed to adhere to the concept of *shram-samman* (reward for labor) rather than *shram-daan* (donation), while staying firm to the principle that even in charity there would be no free lunches.

It was this philosophy that lay the foundation for the 'Cloth for Work' program that has a huge multiplier effect built into its model.

First, it bridges the gap between urban excess and rural scarcity, extending the life of thousands of tons of cloth and other urban surplus. Second, it results in direct savings on new purchases for villagers, leaving them with more disposable income to spend on other urgent needs. Third, it makes villagers self-reliant in addressing local developmental and infrastructure gaps at an extremely low cost because labor is virtually free. It also catalyzes a response from local governments who are incentivized to complete the tasks that villagers have already undertaken. And finally, from Goonj's point of view, it reduces the organization's dependence on monetary donations to carry out developmental work, expediting the scale at which it can effect change.

Today Goonj has an annual operating budget (in cash) of merely ₹20 crores and all of it is raised through donations from corporate partners and individuals. But add to it an approximate monetary value of the 4,000 tons of urban surplus material it collects every year, and an approximate monetary value of the voluntary pro bono labor of rural communities on 4,000 activities every year that it would have incurred traditionally in getting the development work done, and the total working capital of Goonj easily goes up to ₹100 crores. The impact it generates per rupee thus is at least five times its value. And 'Cloth for Work' is the very edifice on which the organization thrives. Its unique incentive structure enhances Goonj's impact manifold, solving not only a material need for clothing but also bringing about massive behavioral changes while reinvigorating local communities.

Teething Pangs

The success wasn't instant though.

A regular non-governmental organization's (NGO's) job would have been limited to collecting and distributing material for the needy. But for Goonj to succeed in its multifarious goals and generate holistic impact at scale, it needed to synchronize several critical parts of a complex supply chain, from collection and processing to distribution and most importantly the last mile developmental effort carried out through 'Cloth for Work' in villages like Pipronia.

Villagers were initially very reluctant to take up on Goonj's offer to work in return for material. They were unsure about whether they would really be given what they were promised, and also had questions about why the organization was interested in intervening sans any missionary or profit motive.

Three decisions helped Goonj tide over this predicament. First, rather than invest precious hours convincing communities of their legitimacy, Anshu decided to hire local staff members in all the regions where Goonj was intervening through 'Cloth for Work' to become part of his team. These staff members, as a result of their familiarity with the beneficiaries, became the de facto liaisons between the organization and the locals, and could be held accountable by the villagers in case of a problem. It gave the communities some much-required confidence.

Second, the positive experience of one village had an immediate cascading effect on other nearby villages, prompting even those who had refused Goonj's offer to intervene initially to come and seek help.

What also helped tremendously was getting villagers to identify their own pain points, i.e., whether to repair a bridge, or build a well, or dig a ditch, rather than dictate to them what they must do. Once they saw that this was going to directly improve their lives, they were happy to come on board.

Goonj tenaciously sourced and deployed local wisdom to appeal to people and it worked in the organization's favor.

But Anshu realized that bringing about these mindset changes only among the villagers wasn't enough. For the government to take responsibility of its own tasks, they needed merely to be the bait, not the fish.

The positive experience of one village had an immediate cascading effect on other nearby villages, prompting even those who had refused Goonj's offer to intervene initially to come and seek help.

"We decided to mobilize people only to get the basics done. What we realized is that once the villagers got the *kaccha* work done, on roads, bridges and wells, they would ensure that the state agencies followed up and made it *pucca* so as to not have their effort go for a waste," explains Anshu. "The state was incentivized to come in, because half their job was done anyway. In that sense, we quickly become the enablers for governance."

Today, the Goonj model has permeated through 24 states and literally thousands of villages. This expansion has only been possible because the organization chose to grow horizontally and develop into an empowered federation of NGOs under one umbrella, rather than remain a single, centralized entity shooting commands from the top.

In order to reach far-flung areas, Anshu began collaborating with a multitude of small organizations across geographies to build a network of partners that included other NGOs, government institutions, the military and individuals. It was a slow brick-by-brick process, but these associations gradually became force multipliers that helped him amplify his effort substantially across different parts of the country and expand quickly using the inorganic route.

This model created a beautiful symbiotic relationship that allowed Goonj to function as a fully decentralized organization with access to local partner intelligence, infrastructure and execution capabilities. Partners on the other hand got materials to carry out developmental tasks which reduced their own dependence on cash and donations. The only expectation was that they adhere to certain common guidelines set by Goonj which were standardized across the board so that the effort could be replicated across locations in a templatized form with minor tweaks.

Instead of a top-down, command-and-control culture where rules were written in stone, NGO partners were asked to follow the broader ethos of the organization but given the flexibility to operate and adapt to local needs

In order to monitor the work being carried out and also organically explore newer areas for intervention, Anshu set up zonal offices staffed with only a few in-house employees. They too were given complete autonomy to take their own decisions but maintained a close, collaborative relationship with the head office. This kept costs in check, and drastically reduced the bureaucracy, even while allowing the organization to quickly expand its footprint geographically.

The Five Ds that Sustain Goonj

All of these front-end strategies at Goonj are underpinned by its strong logistical competency at the backend where tons of material that come in through the day are collected and processed into kits for dispatch across the country.

Today, the cost of delivering a piece of cloth for Goonj is a mere 97 *paisa* and the effort across 24 states is sustained through a very methodical supply chain that works on the five-D principle of **Distribution, Detailing, Direction, Distance and Dignity.**

At its processing center, hidden away in a maze of narrow lanes in Delhi's Sarita Vihar, is a remarkably well-streamlined logistics and **distribution** system. About a hundred women from the nearby slums are hard at work here every day of the week, cleaning, washing, repurposing and repackaging the tons of material that Goonj receives through its sophisticated network of collection centers across the country.

Clothes, shoes, books, furniture, utensils, wedding trousseaus, school bags, stationery, office equipment, musical instruments and even antiques arrive in truckloads at such processing hubs not just in Delhi, but also in Mumbai, Kolkata, Bengaluru, Rishikesh, Hyderabad, Chennai and Kochi. Here these items are carefully coded and sorted so that they can be distributed to communities in kits. A regular 'Cloth for Work' kit comprises the staples—shirts, trousers, sarees, sweaters, a toy, a school bag, utensils, underwear and a bunch of sanitary pads manufactured in-house.

But there are kits also designed to meet specific needs such as a marriage kit or a disaster relief kit or a school kit.

"People generally give what they have, not what people need," says Imran Khan, a core member of the Goonj team who has been around for 12 years. "At these processing centers we try and channelize the material by matching it with people's needs."

This means paying huge attention to the **detailing** process which includes considerations of size, shape, culture, geography, religion and several other factors before deciding which kit will go where. For instance, a kit consisting of *salwar kurtas* will not go to Rajasthan but instead to Punjab. Similarly, shoes with heels will be sent to the plains and not to the hills. Rags and other unusable material will be converted into patchwork quilts. Oversized clothes (according to Anshu, the waist size of the urban male is between 30 and 38 cm while that of the rural male is between 26 and 30 cm) on the other hand will be repurposed to create a diverse range of products such as handbags, cloth folders and decorative knick-knacks that are sold at the distribution centers and retail outlets, generating employment as well as a good ancillary revenue stream for Goonj.

This obsession with the nitty-gritty is what has given the organization minute insight and wisdom to decide also on the **direction** of its efforts.

A regular 'Cloth for Work' kit comprises the staples— shirts, trousers, sarees, sweaters, a toy, a school bag, utensils, underwear and a bunch of sanitary pads manufactured in-house.

Goonj's volunteers, NGO partners and chapter heads working in the field inform the central office of their requirements on a regular basis. These are mapped and monitored through a strict, diligent process in order to avoid lapses and ensure a culture of transparency. Every few months, its national teams also get together to do a strengths, weaknesses, opportunities and threats (SWOT) and impact analysis to see what is working and what is not, share stories of innovation and cross-fertilize ideas.

The organization usually only works either on disaster relief or in the far-flung areas of the country where state agencies do not have a presence. Anshu knew from the very beginning that Goonj needed to have a footprint where nobody had trod in order to reach the most underserved regions in the country, and the aim has always been to build connections and conquer the tyranny of **distance.**

The fifth D binding all of these strands of the complex supply chain is the unwavering commitment to making **dignity** matter. Anshu strongly believes that charity takes away the dignity of the receiver and that without dignity no development is possible. This in an Indian village is of huge consequence, Goonj has learnt over 20 years. Self-respect matters tremendously here, and traditional charities had denied that to the receiver until Goonj came along and challenged the status quo.

A steadfast adherence to this five-D principle ensures that Goonj makes a sustained impact in the long run. It also keeps a tight check on costs and guarantees zero wastage because all the material is repaired and repurposed for something or the other.

In fact, so fastidious is the organization about ensuring that maximum value is derived out of waste that even staples are collected and sold as scrap. And it is this avowed emphasis on thrift and deriving value out of everything that informed and enabled another of Goonj's landmark initiatives, the 'Not Just A Piece of Cloth' or 'My Pad' drive, which allowed it to diversify into the related domain of menstrual hygiene.

'Not Just A Piece of Cloth'

Scale in a social context is as much about getting more bang for your buck by penetrating deeper into a problem as it is about spreading wider and expanding the size of the impact with additional monetary muscle. Goonj's intervention into menstrual hygiene is an example of how it has successfully achieved the former through an almost fanatical culture of thrift and resource optimization.

After rigorously examining the progress on the road building in Pipronia, Chiranjeet Gayen, the chapter head of Goonj in Bundelkhand, summons the women of the village to the grounds of the primary school. Chiranjeet, an alumnus of the Tata Institute of Social Sciences (TISS), is a postgraduate in public health but has been cutting his teeth as a field worker for the past two years with Goonj and heading an important region at the young age of 27.

"I've become a jack of all trades," he says. "But that's all right because the learning has been tremendous, and it's given me a broader perspective that I wouldn't have got had I jumped straight into my niche."

Working on public health issues still gives him a high though, and he is especially in his element when running Goonj's 'Not Just A Piece of Cloth' initiative in the region. Through it, Goonj has been educating women on menstrual hygiene and breaking the taboo over this highly sensitive issue in the country's most socially and economically backward regions by making low-cost pads available to women as a part of the 'Cloth for Work' kits.

'Not Just A Piece of Cloth' is today an essential strand of Goonj's developmental effort, helping it sustain and grow its sphere of influence. To date, nearly 12,00,000 meters of cotton cloth have been converted into five million 'My Pads' and 1,00,000 undergarments and distributed to hundreds of thousands of women across India.

The work began nearly a decade ago when the Goonj team came across a woman who died of tetanus because of a rusted hook in the piece of the blouse she used during her menses. Over the course of the next few years they found that women living in the remote parts of the country used everything from polythene bags to grass, sand, ash and the filthiest rags available because menstruation was in many senses synonymous with dirt for them. Women in the same family with different period cycles often used the same cloth and rarely did they dry it out in the open given the taboos attached. The unhygienic practices made them vulnerable to infection and even deadly diseases like cervical cancer. Many even had to get their uteruses removed at a childbearing age.

It was evidently a monumental crisis that had been simmering across a large section of India for decades, if not centuries and Anshu was appalled that not one of the social organizations working with women had noticed it. He strongly believed that menstruation was a human issue and not a women's issue. Talking to women across the hinterland, he felt that it was critical to break the strong culture of shame and silence around menstruation and normalize it as a biological function.

"There were self-help groups to foster women's entrepreneurship, microfinance institutions to lend money, but none of these NGOs had a budget to address this basic indignity," he says.

Goonj realized that it had ready infrastructure in place to implement a solution. All it needed to do was make low-cost pads from the unusable clothes that came its way at the processing center and distribute them through the 'Cloth for Work' kits. A process was immediately put in place to segregate clothes that were too frayed and tattered and through a rigorous process that put a premium on disinfecting the material, they got converted into the 'My Pad' sanitary napkins.

Implementing the program on the ground was a huge challenge though because it involved broaching a topic that people spoke about only in whispers. "The first time I had to conduct a workshop with the women, I had a nervous breakdown," recalls Chiranjeet. "It took me nearly two hours to explain to the women why this was so important, and why there was no shame in talking about it. But the next time I addressed them, they had begun asking questions."

In Pipronia, Chiranjeet demonstrated the growing enthusiasm for the program by asking the circle of women gathered at the primary school in a roaring voice whether they had any problem talking to him about this because he was a man. "No!" came the response instantly, before the crowd burst into peals of laughter.

It was a moment that reaffirmed how important a modest piece of cloth was in not just giving a woman her rightful dignity but also in opening up a dialogue on a subject that has for long been brushed under the carpet with disastrous consequences on women's health in India.

Anshu credits his team's constant field-level interactions with villagers for recognizing the extent of the problem and thinking up this related diversification without expending additional resources.

A Partner in Disaster

Beyond the issues of poverty and menstruation that warrant Goonj's efforts, it is the organization's seminal work in disaster relief which runs parallel to its regular developmental activities, that has really provided the fuel for its ascent.

In the last 20 years, Goonj has been an integral part of

the relief operations in a series of rehabilitation efforts and has reached lakhs of families with relief kits across states like Assam, Manipur, Bihar, Odisha, West Bengal, Rajasthan, Gujarat, Kerala and Uttarakhand in floods, earthquakes, fires, cyclones and tsunamis. Each of these disasters has proved to be a turning point for the organization.

Goonj's inception in 1999 coincided with a cyclone in Odisha. During the Indian Ocean tsunami in 2004 that hit the coasts of several countries in South and Southeast Asia including India, it spruced up its outreach with Anshu and his family moving out of their home to convert the space into a collection center. The sheer scale of the material that was coming in even forced them to hire another storage space.

Over the next few years, Anshu consistently worked in this sphere, travelling into the remotest parts of the country to gradually equip himself with subtle but invaluable nuances of good disaster management, and closely tracked patterns in disaster preparedness.

By 2008, Goonj had a formalized structure for its disaster operations and streamlined processes to cope with any emergency, becoming the default partners to agencies working on relief and rehabilitation. During the Kosi floods that year, its strong network of local communities and partners helped it rapidly accelerate disaster response.

The organization gained critical mass during the floods in Uttarakhand in 2013, collecting a staggering ₹20 crores in donations. "This was more than our entire turnover for the last 13 years," says Anshu. "Our systems collapsed, payment gateway crashed and for the very first time I realized that we were being perceived as a big, important agency during relief operations. Just after the disaster, from three–four contributions a day, we had 1200–1500 people sending money for some days."

The team had to go into a quick huddle and lay out a strategy to effectively manage the volumes, introducing sophisticated coding, generating automatic receipts and expanding its presence by adding new offices across other cities.

A big reason for Goonj's success in disaster relief is that its efforts here almost seamlessly dovetail into the daily developmental work it carries out across the country, feeding off the strengths of the large infrastructure it has created over the years.

Goonj is able to quickly tap into its massive urban and rural network of stakeholders and 250 grassroots partner organizations when disaster strikes, giving it a unique first-mover advantage. The networks are activated intensely and instantly during such times, and provide timely, accurate assessments of the damage far more quickly than the teams of centralized NGOs.

"We've literally laid an optical fiber across India through our network of NGOs," says Anshu. "They've made us nimble-footed and we can put into action any operation through a ready network of urban schools, collages, corporates, volunteers, Resident Welfare Associations (RWAs) and in rural India—youth groups, volunteers, NGOs, the army, paramilitary forces, etc.— whether a call comes from Kashmir or Kanyakumari."

Goonj also has a clear tactical approach during such times of emergency. Contrary to the first in last out approach of other organizations, it enters only after the arc lights have dimmed, the chaos has died down, the media has disappeared and the time has come for the rescue effort to give way to relief and rehabilitation. It uses the time immediately after a disaster to garner as many resources as possible from across India and to set up base and build local teams and collaborations. "Other agencies make the effort of going in immediately sometimes with help that is not immediately needed. But we've realized, that's not effective, as those competencies lie only with the army, or people who are specially trained," explains Anshu.

Last but not least, the wisdom Goonj has acquired over 20 years comes in handy in deciding the nature of the response which Anshu believes is critical during these times. "We know when to give, what to give and how much to give. Over the years we've realized for instance, that a second pair of clothes becomes a liability during times of disaster, because the basic thing that people have lost is storage space."

All of this aside, the social media-savvy team at Goonj has done a consistently phenomenal job of communicating their requirements effectively, which explains why platforms like Facebook have used it as a case study on how to use social media during a disaster.

"I make sure I get back to the ground in times of cataclysmic events like these," says Anshu, who has often spent months stationed in Nepal, Uttarakhand, Odisha and other places, building local teams who sustain the relief effort once Goonj leaves. "It's a humbling experience," he says, and a much-needed reminder of his purpose, given how easy it is to lose sight of it amid the applause and awards that continually come his way these days.

The Next Big Leap

Over the years, Anshu has received top national and global awards, including the Ashoka Fellowship, the Schwab Foundation's Social Entrepreneur of the Year Award in 2012, and most notably, the Ramon Magsaysay Award in 2015. Flattering press coverage and high-profile appearances on television, including on shows like *Kaun Banega Crorepati* (*KBC*), have followed.

"We got 500 truckloads of material after the *KBC* episode aired," he says, explaining the impact this appearance has had on the public perception around Goonj. "And while I am thrilled, I am also a bit worried that our awards have started becoming a bit of a liability as every time people read about us or see us on television, unlike other organizations we get more material but not parallel monetary inputs."

It's an honest admission of a strange predicament that Goonj finds itself in today, 20 years into its existence, and at the cusp of adulthood.

It was once an organization that prided itself on the fact that it didn't solicit money. But as the scale of its logistical operations grows, it requires more cash than what is currently coming in to process the material. So, the very element that once put it on the path to success has now created a perception problem for the brand.

"When people hear of other charities, they send money. When they hear of us, they only send clothes. This mindset needs to change," admits Anshu. Not one to shy away from change, Goonj is starting to talk to the masses about why money matters along with the material.

It is going to be interesting to observe what this predicament does to the partnerships it has forged with corporate donors.

So far, Goonj has insisted on setting up terms and conditions that promote a relationship of equality between the organization and a corporate donor who might want to come on board. Anshu believes that if big businesses could do what Goonj does simply by using their money might, they would not approach him in the first place. And so, he has been intolerant of a big brother donor-centric approach, preferring to work only with like-minded partners who understand why he does what he does. The question that now emerges is: will such exacting values be maintained or are they at the risk of dilution?

> Local leaders and satraps at some places are not exactly comfortable with an outside agency helping people who are otherwise beholden to them as that diminishes their importance.

Another existential issue that the organization confronts as its sphere of influence increases is the resistance from officials at the grassroots and from local influencers who are conceivably threatened by its ability to persuade communities to take matters into their own hands. Local leaders and satraps at some places are not exactly comfortable with an outside agency helping people who are otherwise beholden to them as that diminishes their importance. However, since its work is not concentrated in one region and there is still a lot of ground left for it to cover this may not be an immediate cause to lose sleep over.

As he looks towards the next 20 years, Anshu is clear that he does not want to grow the organization anymore in terms of consciously expanding teams or office space. What he wants to do instead is grow Goonj as an idea. "I am giving people a copyright to copy us. Everything is open source, and I invite people to come and learn from us so that they can do better, innovate more, add more depth and wisdom," he says.

Some may see this as a deeply altruistic approach but for

Anshu, it is pragmatism that drives the philosophy behind it. Given how enormous our developmental challenges are, he believes that more people have got to be involved, the volumes have to increase and using the Goonj model as a successful prototype can only help in spreading the idea further.

"Ours is a revolutionary economic concept. We began using cloth or material as currency, but expand that idea and imagine what would happen if people began using labor and wisdom as currency for development?" Anshu observes.

It is indeed a compelling question to brood over as we wait for Goonj to grow from an organization into a replicable idea that spawns more offshoots over the next 20 years.

Sutras to Creating, Sustaining and Scaling Innovation:
Business Insights from the Goonj Journey

By highlighting clothing as a basic need, repositioning it as a developmental resource and developing a parallel economy to spread its vast reach across India, Goonj has radically changed the vocabulary of what it means to be a developmental organization with its three-pronged intervention. And it has clearly adhered to at least five of the seven sutras or principles distilled by us to scale its innovation.

Organization	Gap in the Market, Market in the Gap?	Flexible Approach	Customer Centricity	Capital Consciousness	Hiring – Passion over Pedigree	Culture of Innovation	Amplification of Vision
Goonj			✓	✓	✓	✓	✓

Customer Centricity: Goonj's fierce focus on the end user is displayed through several of its mottos. The undertaking to bring about an attitudinal shift in the act of giving from the donor's pride to the receiver's dignity has been underpinned by a process that works to carefully assess and give its beneficiaries exactly what they need rather than what a donor offers. So instead of a uniform one-size-fits-all approach, Goonj carefully channelizes material, keeping geographical, cultural and situational nuances in mind.

Capital Consciousness: Thrift is not second but first nature to Goonj whose very operating model is hinged upon using as little cash as possible to scale up its impact. It has been able to successfully achieve this at multiple levels:

- By bringing back the age-old tradition of barter, giving old material in exchange for labor instead of cash.

- By optimizing every resource and even earning an ancillary income by repurposing the rags that cannot be donated into usable items for sale.

- By conserving cash in every possible way. For instance, in all its years of operations, it claims to have never bought a sheet of paper for administrative paperwork. Goonj does all its correspondence using the unused side of letter pads, leaflets, reports, etc. that are donated to its processing centers. The goal is to spend as little money as possible on its own infrastructure, including tables, chairs, computers and other administrative needs.

The advantages of this obsession with frugality cannot be overemphasized. As has been explained earlier, Goonj is able to generate five times more impact per rupee than other charities reliant upon monetary donations because of its ingenious operating model.

Hiring – Passion over Pedigree: Goonj has close to 1,000 employees including daily wage community workers along with its processing team on its payroll who get employee benefits. They are hired not on the basis of how qualified they are but how hungry they are to make a change. As a result, Goonj has people from all backgrounds working for it, from ex-corporate executives to those who have studied social work and even field-level workers who do not have a formalized educational background but come equipped with a strong knowledge of the local milieu as well as requisite language skills.

Goonj consciously hires only through referrals from friends and family. This works because the new entrants then have a shared value system and the person who is referring them already knows if they will survive in this unique working environment. Anshu believes that an idea can be developed only if employees become co-drivers in filtering the founder's vision down the ranks. And for that to happen, passion is infinitely more critical than pedigree.

Culture of Innovation: Most of Goonj's processes and product innovations are driven by its teams who have their ears and eyes on the ground and not by the head office. Teams collate feedback from beneficiaries and partners and proactively implement it without fear. Anshu has created a nourishing environment for teams to be innovative by taking the following measures:

- Regional teams are given full flexibility to operate and adapt to local scenarios, drastically reducing organizational bureaucracy.

- The mantra that has been communicated to teams is, "Do not take what is given to you as gospel; you must apply your own mind to it based on what you see on the ground." The diversity of environments in which Goonj operates makes a one-size-fits-all approach redundant.

- Regional heads from across the country are brought down to the head office every quarter to share new learnings with each other in a bid to cross-fertilize ideas and replicate projects that have been successful in one part of the country elsewhere.

Team feedback and insights are taken very seriously and members are given the chance to experiment with their ideas and implement them on the ground through pilots. Goonj believes that it is critical to derive first-hand understanding of every unique environment and refuses to blindly implement textbook strategies given by experts that are based on experiences in other scenarios.

Amplification of Vision: Goonj has done this in many ways. It has been successful in building upon its flagship programs like 'Cloth for Work' with valuable add-ons such as the 'My Pad' initiative. It is a great example of how social response can be multiplied with creative addendums, and without expending additional resources. It is an allied activity that ties in with the larger principle but solves a completely different and perhaps more pressing need.

Goonj has now set its ambition to transform from being an organization to a movement and it is taking efforts in this direction by making its knowledge an open source and creating a "copyright to copy kit".

But beyond these five sutras, an essential factor unique to Goonj that has helped it grow from a strappy start-up to a market leader is a strong network of partnerships.

Goonj is not a centralized command-and-control entity but a federation of several loose organizations. It is not trying to do everything on its own. Given the scale of the challenge before him, Anshu realized early on that he needed to take a collaborative approach to expansion.

Today Goonj's presence across 24 states and thousands of villages can only be sustained due to its partnerships and collaborative networks in cities and villages across India. This has enabled it to attract and retain thousands of volunteers from the community who work on the gigantic task of collecting and distributing 4,000 tons of waste material. Affiliations, according to the Stanford Social Innovation Review, can be a critical tool for "spreading impact" and offers non-profits the "broadest range of possibilities". Such an operating model is broadly defined by its ability to bring several independent entities under one brass umbrella to replicate the effort jointly at a much larger scale while allowing them significant autonomy in their functioning.

This model has in some sense already helped

Goonj inch towards its next target of becoming a widespread movement. Can it cover the distance between an NGO and a non-governmental movement (NGM)—a real yardstick of scale in the social sector? The next few years will show.

3

Rivigo

Making Logistics Human with Deep Tech

It was on a solo road trip in 2014 on the back of a trailer truck that Deepak Garg had an epiphany about what is today Rivigo, India's first $1 billion logistics start-up that is perceptibly disrupting the way the country moves freight with its unique 'driver relay' model.

An Indian Institute of Technology (IIT Kanpur) and Indian Institute of Management (IIM Lucknow) alumnus, 32-year-old Garg was comfortably embedded in a high-flying career with the world's most prestigious consulting firm Mckinsey & Company at the time. He was blissfully unschooled in the grueling ways of the trucking and logistics business, but had a desperate desire to do something entrepreneurial. He wanted to do something that would create real social and economic impact, something far removed from his sanitary multinational corporation (MNC) existence.

Logistics seemed like the perfect fit. It was a sunrise sector, on the cusp of a massive transformation. The Goods and

Services Tax (GST) was in the pipeline, and the government was making all the effort it could to modernize logistics-related infrastructure which was plagued by concerns around high costs, low technology adoption and glaring inefficiencies in system facilitates that were impeding the seamless movement of goods within the country.

About 70 percent of freight in India was transported by roads, but in the $160 billion trucking industry there was a crying need for help at every level of the value chain—from fragmented fleet owners who owned less than five trucks and made up over 80 percent of the market, hapless drivers who were leaving trucking by the hoards because of grueling working conditions to customers who bore the brunt of the systemic rot in the form of unreliable, tardy service. It presented an opportunity to create impact at scale.

"I had been studying the space closely, and was toying with a tech-logistics kind of idea like many others at the time, wondering what disruptive technologies could be deployed to revolutionize the bricks-and-mortar business," recalls Garg. "But I didn't just want to replicate a globally successful me-too model back in India."

While hunting for inspiration, which was taking its sweet time to come, a trip to Jaipur with an NGO, in the deep summer of 2014 to distribute pillow covers to an organization, gave Garg the brainwave that was eluding him in Delhi.

"In Jaipur I met a driver at a Highway Seva Kendra, who told me that drivers were considered the 37th caste—the lowest in the pecking order of India's caste gradations. They lived away from home for months on end in terrible conditions. Forty percent of the trucking families had HIV, 25 percent didn't get married and on an average a truck driver lived a life that was ten years shorter than a regular human being," says Garg.

Garg heard horror stories from hundreds of truck drivers over the course of the next few days. "A *sardarji* from Punjab told me he had met his son only five times in his life, because he'd spent his entire existence behind the wheel of a trailer truck," he narrates.

The close-quarter ground interactions with drivers belied all his armchair research, fundamentally altering his world view of logistics. And the new insights he had gathered from the ground made him revisit the very problem he was setting out to address.

The most elemental issue with logistics, Garg realized on that trip, was not operations, processing inefficiencies or cost optimization as was the commonly held belief in the start-up world that was busy crafting breakneck technology solutions to tackle these pain points. It was a more pressing and deep-rooted issue that concerned the devastating lives of the truck drivers and threatened to put the very sustenance of the industry in peril.

For every 1,000 trucks on the road, there were only 780 drivers available to drive them according to the government's own statistics. And that number was expected to go down to 480 by 2020, leading to a chronic paucity of those choosing trucking as a career. This could potentially cripple the backbone of the Indian economy if something was not done urgently to improve their lives.

The one-day trip to Jaipur quickly extended to a week-long journey. Garg cancelled his plans of coming back to Delhi and travelled with the men of the road, hearing more poignant tales of desperation and crushed dreams. He finally got off at Vapi, where on the banks of the Daman Ganga river, he had his moment of revelation. Logistics, he realized, had to be made more humane.

The trucker had to be put at the center of the change desired, aided by a strong interplay of technology, data, culture and operational excellence. And the way to do it would be through a global first idea in trucking called the 'driver relay', by which every driver would come back to the comfort of his home each night, and regain a life of meaning, respect and dignity—basic human needs that had been overlooked for decades by a moribund industry that had not considered the social or economic costs of its human neglect.

The Brainwave

Entrepreneurs waste money and energy all too often, trying to reinvent the wheel. But Garg's idea was not new at all. The relay system was in use for centuries. In the early 1300s, King Edward I of England had purportedly instituted a relay mechanism for horses to carry couriers to other provinces. It was used in rail transportation networks for decades, and the airlines too adopted it for their pilot rosters. What Garg was seeking to do was merely transpose an existing practice from one segment of the transport business into another.

The trucks would be passed on as batons in a relay race where a driver would hand over his truck to the next driver at the end of his shift. Pitstops would be set up along a particular route, and a changeover would happen every few hours so that a driver could return to his home destination, driving back the truck coming from the opposite direction.

He could see the immediate benefits of his idea.

Limiting the distance a driver drove would ensure that he came back home every evening. This would go a long way in addressing the issues of poor health, substance abuse and safety as he would be able to spend more time in his natural social environment, eat home-cooked meals, sleep in his own bed and save some money. All of this would lead to a direct improvement in his quality of life.

Nights in particular constitute 40–50 percent of the total journey time in the trucking supply chain leading to sub-optimal usage of the vehicle.

Traditionally a single driver covers the entire distance between two destinations with intermittent halts along the way for rest which significantly derails delivery speeds. Nights in particular constitute 40–50 percent of the total journey time in the trucking supply chain leading to sub-optimal usage of the vehicle. The relay would however completely eliminate the down time. The asset (or the truck) would sweat to the fullest because the trucks would run 22–23 hours in a day, reducing the idle hours substantially.

And this would lead to a concomitant reduction in delivery time, vastly improving reliability and customer experience.

The need of the market was also hefty. There was a demand for a million truck drivers every year, or 10 percent of the nation's employment agenda, if one considered the fact that ten million young Indians were entering the workforce annually. And Garg was convinced that if he could convert his idea into reality, it would decidedly encourage more people to join this line of work and attack the problem of attrition head on.

"I was always inspired to use a business solution to solve a real social problem rather than doing it via CSR or NGOs.

And given the efficiencies this model brought at all levels at least on paper, I was convinced that I could make money from it, while also significantly altering the lives of people, and the way the industry functioned," says Garg.

It was a disruptive idea that could be both a money spinner and a social game changer. But back in Delhi after his weeklong journey, his father was livid. "How could a Mckinsey guy want to have anything to do with trucks?" he thundered, upset that his highly-qualified son would even consider dabbling in a crude, unorganized business like trucking. And for three months thereafter they didn't speak a word to one another.

But Garg was fully charged up, his mind roused by the great potential the idea held. And so, despite fierce opposition from the family, he quit his job to enter the start-up battlefield to chase his entrepreneurial dream.

Two to Tango

Some 12,000 km away from Delhi, Gazal Kalra, an ex-McKinsey colleague of Garg's from another department, who was also his close friend's wife, was finishing her double Masters degrees in Business and Public Administration from Stanford University and the Harvard Kennedy School of Government. Despite her enviable academic pedigree, she too, like him wanted to get her hands dirty in business and solve "fundamental problems back home".

Barely days after her return to India, Kalra's husband spoke to her about Garg's decision to quit McKinsey, the trip to Jaipur that had inspired him to take that leap of faith and suggested that the two meet to bounce off ideas.

"I met him a few days later at a Café Coffee Day where he

told me he was looking to build an Uber-like platform for truckers. My initial reaction was an eye roll," admits Kalra. "I was just back from the valley where everyone had latched on to this trend, trying to crack an Uber for something! I said to myself, god, he's one of those!"

But Garg convinced her that his wasn't merely yet another vanilla technology solution crafted in a vacuum. The relay innovation would fundamentally solve the human problem in the value chain and put the truck driver at the very center of the ecosystem.

The potency of the idea lay in the fact that it had identified conceivably the biggest pain point of the industry overlooked by a bevy of entrepreneurs eager to push technology into the market without an understanding of the profound socio-cultural complexities of the sector. Here was a business wanting to use it to break through a very real, tough-to-crack social problem that could transform logistics quite dramatically. It was precisely the kind of monumental, long-gestation challenge that Kalra was hungry to partake in.

"I was absolutely inspired and thought, if there was something worth trying in life, it was this. Even if it failed, I could look back and be proud of it. I told Garg to stop calling it an Uber-like platform for trucking because he was short selling the idea by doing that. This was something more profound," she says.

The idea held an emotional appeal for Kalra. Her father was in the army and posted away from home for long intervals. He was sent to Sri Lanka when she was barely a few months old and only returned after she had turned two and a half. She had grown up with her mother showing her the emotional letters they exchanged during the long bouts of separation. She could feel the pain of the drivers, who spent between 20–25 days away from home every month, often at the risk of weakening their familial bonds.

"The problem statement was quite simple: How do we bring the driver back home every evening? The solution—to limit the distance he travelled. And the way to do it was through a relay, enabled by cutting-edge technology that would envision the truck as an IoT platform fitted with trackers, sensors and responsive real-time logistics," explains Kalra.

It would not only change the lives of drivers but also bring significant benefits to customers by reducing delivery time.

Both she and Garg had confidence that at least on paper the idea held the promise to create great magic in the lives of two key stakeholders in the business—the trucker and the customer. But executing this deceptively straightforward plan was no mean feat as the duo would find out over the course of the following few months.

Hitting the Ground Running

Deep faith in their revolutionary pitch and a fair bit of madness were the only two things that Garg and Kalra had going for them as they lunged into a territory that bore little resemblance to the plush, air-conditioned tranquil of their erstwhile corporate lives.

The challenges seemed insurmountable at first. On the external front the duo truly began to grasp what the term 'poor transport ecosystem' meant in the Indian context. Pitiable road infrastructure, bureaucratic quagmires at check posts in a pre-GST world, patchy smartphone and data penetration, low-capacity truck usage and technological illiteracy, they realized, could seriously imperil their dream even before it got off the ground.

Internally, the usual start-up hardships stared them in the face including lack of money, insufficient human resources, a sea of opposition and other teething organizational troubles.

"But when you have a great idea, you start living and breathing the power of that idea. And that propels you to do crazy things and gives you the energy to fight against all the odds," says Kalra, remembering the initial days when they started out in the National Capital Region (NCR), interviewing truck drivers for their first pilot project in the middle of nowhere in June when the North Indian summer was at its peak.

"Despite a whole lot of people telling us we were much too educated to be doing what we were setting out to do, friends and well-wishers cautioning me against deeply misogynistic working conditions in the logistics business and potential investors questioning every decision of ours from not replicating a tried-and-tested model that had worked in the US or having an application ready before we tested the waters, we went right ahead with our plans," says Kalra.

This belief came from several rounds of informal conversations with truck drivers at resting pitstops, hole-in-the-wall highway restaurants and fuel stations outside Delhi. They all said the idea would be a hit because it had quite accurately understood their most pertinent predicament.

That was enough of a catalyst for them to register their company, Trucks First on August 11, 2014.

But that was the first mistake. No smart, educated person wanted to join a trucking start-up. They realized that and within months renamed the company Rivigo, to symbolize the movement of a flowing river that conquers all hurdles to bring freedom, growth and transformation—principles that would define the company's business ethos.

Garg and Kalra truly embraced the 'head in the clouds, feet on the ground' approach as they began laying the groundwork for the relay. While the grand purpose of 'making logistics human' anchored them, their journey really began by working on the nuts and bolts, carefully listening to the truckers' stories, understanding their frustrations and aspirations, and taking quick, practical action to make iterations to their business model by incorporating the feedback they received from the ground.

They renamed the company 'Rivigo' to symbolize the movement of a flowing river that conquers all hurdles to bring freedom, growth and transformation—principles that would define the company's business ethos.

They held what they called 'driver sabhas', huddles at halting places along highway routes near Delhi where they could catch hold of hundreds of drivers at once and carry out effective outreach. They would also traverse the *dhabas* or highway eateries that are common meeting spots for truck drivers in the periphery of the NCR to have casual meetings with them. Here they would explain their idea over a cup of tea, testing the response to it, establishing networks to start hiring and extracting as much ground wisdom as possible.

For instance, detailed discussions with drivers about their recommended model of trucks was used as feedback to decide on what fleet they would buy. Eye-opening disclosures about how a driver's family life and health were affected as a result of being away from home for long periods at a stretch led to the design of the relay model that ensured that every driver would be behind the wheel for only 8–10 hours a day and reach home by night, no matter what.

On the side, they also set up a call center asking drivers who wanted to be employed to get in touch for more details. They distributed pamphlets on highways in the NCR and ran a referral program through which they got nearly 2,000 leads in a matter of a few months.

Simultaneously they also rolled out a pitstop network and began readying a team to conduct the first pilot.

"We had really begun empathizing with the truck drivers, and understanding them better," says Kalra. Understanding their pain gave the duo the ignition required to buttress their own belief in their idea and also the fuel to execute it despite the challenges.

Equipped with great ground-level insights, it did not take them long to clinch the first round of angel funding to get things off the ground.

Seeding the Idea

How Rivigo raised its first bit of seed money is in fact an interesting story. They had already been rejected by a number of investors when in mid-2014 Garg happened to meet with the then-chairman of Singapore Post, Lim Ho Kee, during a trip to Singapore. A very successful business leader of Chinese origins, he was fascinated with Garg's pitch and during the course of their conversation casually asked him whether his favorite character from the *Mahabharata* was Arjuna or Karna.

"I said to him that while both were warriors of equal

strength and bravery, I would, however, go with Karna, because he was a giver," says Garg.[1] That did it. SingPost was impressed and went on to invest in the angel round. Along with some personal capital and help from a few friends of Garg at McKinsey, the initial funding needs were taken care of.

Operations began with two trucks and Rivigo signing up as a vendor to Gati, the courier services major to get a first-hand experience of the business. Their first trip was between Pataudi (near Delhi) and Pune and it gave them a precise idea of the nature of the challenges they would encounter over the years as they set out to transform logistics.

The truck broke down on that trip because the driver stole fuel and mixed it with kerosene. All their planning went for a toss as a result.[2] But the incident gave Garg and Kalra a sense of the multiple moving pieces in the industry that they would need to fix simultaneously as they set out on their own.

By August 2014, with the money Rivigo had raised, it set up a small office in Gurgaon, bought its first 15 trucks and onboarded 24 drivers or 'pilots' as they were called. And by Diwali that year, in less than two months of launching operations, the company was ready to make its first delivery through its own relay network.

This was a period when e-commerce—a time-sensitive industry that promised high speed deliveries—was just taking off in India, and Rivigo piggybacked on that growth. One of its first big orders was from Flipkart during the Big Billion Day Sale where the e-commerce major could not do its quick deliveries because air capacity was choked. It was an important Diwali for them and they were sending everything by air because their supply chain had been disrupted as a result of the delays. Rivigo took advantage of the situation, made a cold call to Flipkart and asked them to try out their service.

And so, a trip between Mumbai and Delhi was scheduled on the route on which the company had laid out a pitstop network for its pilots whereby a change of drivers could happen every 4–5 hours at Jaipur, Hindwara, Baroda, Vapi and finally Mumbai.

The journey that usually took up to 52 hours was completed in less than 26 hours on Rivigo's relay. And Flipkart's entire warehouse was waiting outside to receive the truck that had traversed the distance without delay or breakdown. It was an unprecedented feat! Less than six months after they had begun operations, Kalra and Garg had demonstrated that they had the ability to translate their idea from paper to reality.

Journey to Scale

By April 2015, following several successful delivery trials on the relay, Rivigo approached SAIF Partners who decided to put in close to $10 million in the company in a Series A funding round. In December 2015, SAIF invested another $30 million in a Series B round, followed by Warburg Pincus picking up a minority stake for $75 million in November 2016. A year later, Rivigo closed a $50 million funding round led by both SAIF and Warburg Pincus jointly.

Today, barely five years since it was founded, Rivigo has inched close to the coveted unicorn status with post-money valuation of nearly $1 billion and the monetary heft to really begin creating impact at scale.

Apart from marquee names like Flipkart and Amazon who are today Rivigo's biggest customers, the firm boasts of a client list of 2,000-plus large enterprises/businesses spread across sectors ranging from pharmaceuticals and dairy to frozen foods, consumer goods and textiles. Its revenues in FY17 zoomed to ₹402 crores with 3,000 trucks in its fleet and more or less those many people on its payroll. From one operating route between Delhi and Mumbai, Rivigo's trucks today ply across India on 26 lanes and over 70 pitstops, having vastly improved the lives of thousands of truck drivers.

It also owns 200 processing centers around the country and has expanded to offering part-truck loads, setting up a feeder network of smaller trucks.

In addition to setting up the relay network, in 2016, Rivigo launched a digital freight marketplace, connecting carriers (truck fleet) with spot buyers (customers who wished to transport their goods) in a non-relay set up.

This is basically an application that can be used by any fleet owner and customer across any part of the country to connect demand with supply for a small commission. It is like an Uber or an Ola service but instead of the cab there is a truck with a businessman who wants to transport his goods. Unlike with its relay service, the trucks are not owned by Rivigo and neither do they have to ply on its designated relay network. It is a wider service that digitally connects supply and demand for third party vendors at the best available price. And that has already captured 10 percent of the market with over one million trucks on the platform.

The company's brisk pace of growth is impressive on its own. But what makes it more remarkable is that it has achieved this feat while at least a dozen logistics start-ups went out of business.

And this begs the question: what is it that the duo did differently from the others that enabled them to scale in a sector riddled with enormous execution complexities?

The Making of an Outlier

Logistics is a business that offered start-ups tremendous scope for growth and had low barriers to entry, attracting a plethora of entrepreneurs in 2013 who wanted to put technology to work to solve a range of inefficiencies from documentation processes to reduced idle hours for trucks and easy payments.

While technology is the backbone of Rivigo's operations today, the critical mistake that Garg and Kalra avoided was first rolling out technology and then building their product. "We first piloted the relay to see if the life of a truck driver really changed. It is only once we tested the impact of the product on the ground, and perfected it that we began focusing on the tech aspect of it," says Kalra.

This approach allowed Rivigo to really get a grip on the basic legacy issues that plagued the sector and offer clients a different product that was virtually tailor-made for the Indian context, prompting them to make that sticky move from cheaper unorganized fleet services to the premium offering by Rivigo.[3]

A number of start-ups failed because they "did not take a full stack view of the Indian logistics sector. Just adding a thin layer of technology does not solve the deep-rooted problems such as non-availability of drivers and fragmented truck ownership," said Mukul Arora, managing director, SAIF Partners.[4]

Rivigo's USP lay in the fact that it attacked the deep-rooted problems of driver wellbeing, optimal asset utilization and transparency at the very core, and dramatically altered the service experience for all the key stakeholders in the supply chain. While the truck driver's life saw vast improvements due to the relay, for customers it boiled down to tangible improvements in delivery speed and a visible price advantage.

Over the years, Rivigo claims to have reduced cargo delivery time by 60–70 percent because the relay system allows its fleet to remain on the road 24/7, even during the nights, which is a significant differentiation. And while it charges a small premium to the market price, it says clients see a saving of between 10–20 percent in logistics costs when they move to Rivigo because its trucks do not return empty and that cost-benefit is passed on to the consumer.

"In transport, fixed cost is around 45 percent to 50 percent, whether a truck runs for 10 km or 100 km. While trucks in the traditional model do about three trips a month, Rivigo's trucks do about seven return trips," says Manish Saigal, managing director at advisory firm Alvarez & Marsal and a leading sector expert.[5]

Also, unlike the old, poorly-maintained, tarpaulin-covered trucks that exposed cargo to vulnerabilities, Rivigo introduced a fleet of containerized, tech-enabled trucks that gave clients added safety and tracking visibility, both deep-seated challenges in the traditional setup.

A common mistake many entrepreneurs make in their innovation journey is that they go to the market with ready-made solutions. It was Albert Einstein who famously said, "If I had an hour to solve a problem, I'd spend 55 minutes thinking about the problem and five minutes thinking about solutions". Few take the wisdom in this adage seriously. But can you really solve something if you don't have a full grip on what it is that you are trying to solve?

According to Darrel Mann, CTO of the consulting agency Blackswan and former engineer at Rolls-Royce, who has spent a considerable amount of time studying innovation flops, "25 percent of failures were due to people trying to solve the wrong problems". Defining a problem, he adds, "clearly and completely represents 90 percent of the difficulty in innovation".[6]

Garg's and Kalra's efforts to do a complete deep-dive into the problem by intently listening to and engaging with it became a fundamental ingredient to their initial success. It allowed them to identify the most pronounced pain points and find precise solutions rather than retrofitting generic me-too ideas that would yield only incremental benefits to its stakeholders.

Swimming against the Tide

In fact, this deep-dive approach is what informed Rivigo's decision to employ an asset-heavy, ownership-led business model to begin with, and use the bricks-and-mortar learnings to transition to a technology-backed aggregation model. Rivigo took this bold, counterintuitive decision even though Garg's initial ambition was to build an Uber-like platform for trucking and marketplace aggregation was the buzzword in the market.

"After my close-quarter interactions with people in the business, I realized that you can't build a marketplace if you don't know how to run trucks, can't understand the pain of supplier and operator, or manage expenses, tyres, spare parts, bookings, etc. If you are not that guy you will not be able to build a successful aggregation platform. This is not like cab aggregation. It is far more complex, and we needed to learn the ropes," says Garg.

Rivigo today owns a fleet of 3,000 trucks but has a grand mission to eventually have every truck on the road run on a relay system. Clearly it cannot own all the trucks in the country. It will need to onboard outside fleet owners to use its relay platform as a service. But for them to buy the idea, it was incumbent upon the founders to first put their money where their mouth was and prove to themselves and to the ecosystem that the concept could actually work on the ground.

"We had to establish the ecosystem, build the technology and test it on various parameters before we could be confident of providing the same level of service through aggregation. For that, it was important that we had our own fleet," says Garg. "Today, I can conclusively say that both the customer and the pilot (or driver) believe in the relay."

Currently two separate entities operate under the Rivigo umbrella—the relay business in which it owns the fleet that plies only on its pitstop network and the non-relay freight marketplace platform where it does not own the fleet but provides nearly one million users a platform with freight load and smartphones, connecting external fleet owners to the demand all around the country.

A small textile enterprise in Ludhiana wanting to send a consignment to Lucknow can simply register on the marketplace, get quotes from trucking companies willing to do the trip, choose their desired vendor and transport the goods.

The fundamentals of this non-relay freight marketplace are quite similar to the business model of the taxi aggregators, except that in this case it is used by truckers rather than cabdrivers at one end, and enterprises rather than commuters at the other. Just like Uber or Ola provide a technology platform or an application to their driver partners and end-users, Rivigo does the same to disaggregated truckers and companies across the country.

By next year it will also begin piloting a 'relay as a service' concept through the aggregation platform where truck fleets not owned by Rivigo will be able to relay through the Rivigo network using an application. This is where the opportunity to apply the relay concept across the whole trucking economy and achieve exponential scale lies.

"It's been a gradual evolution year by year and going as per plan," says Garg. "In 2014, we started the relay with our own assets. Then we built the freight marketplace where we will grow from one million (user base) to four million. And now we are ready to launch 'relay as a service' which will vastly expand the market without requiring much capital outlay."

The fundamentals of this non-relay freight marketplace are quite similar to the business model of the taxi aggregators, except that in this case it is used by truckers rather than cabdrivers at one end, and enterprises rather than commuters at the other.

Rivigo's own expansion of physical assets will not extend beyond 5,000 trucks, says Garg, as the company evolves into a relay marketplace.

"Capital will be prioritized for building high-quality technology to scale the business over owning physical assets. We will buy physical assets only if we need to, but not for operational reasons. For example, if there is a project where I need to buy 100 trucks but don't see the value of those 100 trucks from the point of view of building or testing technology for relay as a service, then I will not buy them," he adds, stating that owning the asset is no longer critical because the company has over the years built sophisticated technology and automation processes using data science and deep analytics that will ensure that the same level of service quality is delivered even on the aggregator platform where it does not own the fleet.

"There are no physical touch points on any of our 3,000 trucks currently. The algorithms, using complex analytics, machine learning and AI tools do all the decision-making, from when the truck should go to the fuel pump, or for credit maintenance to the actual pricing. Everything is digital. And that's what technology does. It eliminates the quality margin between owning a truck and not owning it, because the decision making is not in the hands of the human being," explains Garg.

Technology is at the very epicenter of everything that Rivigo does today. While the founders' initial focus was rightfully on creating a holistic ecosystem for the relay rather than merely adding a 'thin layer of technology', they were always convinced that their mission to make logistics human at scale would have to be enabled by cutting-edge technology.

Driven by Tech

Rivigo's head office, a four-storied steel-and-glass structure in the heart of Gurugram, with funky wall murals and inspiring blow-up quotes of Steve Jobs has a cool, edgy vibe that is hard to miss. Here, hundreds of nerdy young techies are immersed in writing high-quality codes to track the thousands of trucks crisscrossing the country and using artificial intelligence to solve complex problems of allocation, pilferage, efficient utilization, price discovery, etc.

One of the key differentiators between Rivigo and the scores of other logistics players who outsource their technology piece to established companies is that the former has over these years obsessively built from scratch a formidable array of in-house proprietary tech solutions to address every possible problem on a truck journey. At last count it had developed as many as 50 products, from multi-lingual chatbots to fuel pilferage detection systems and geo-location sensors, giving its offering an unrivaled edge.

Fuel is conceivably the biggest operating expense in the logistics industry, making up 40–45 percent of the overall cost of delivery, and the ingenuity with which Rivigo has stopped its rampant theft and misuse is illustrative of how it has been crafting deep-tech solutions to surmount age-old challenges.

It has developed what it calls 'in-house diagnostic engines and dashboards' that detect fuel pilferage with 100 percent accuracy. Through raw data analysis and using advanced mathematical and statistical modelling these perceive even the slightest drop in the fuel levels which come in as red alerts for action.

Additionally, it has identified parameters like average speed, vehicle idling, over speeding and speed volatility to track the fuel efficiency of drivers. The most efficient drivers can get about 30 percent better fuel efficiency than the least efficient ones if they improve their driving behavior based on these parameters.

The impact of its technological interventions is visible thus not just in huge cost savings but more importantly better fuel efficiency and driving behavior.

While the relay sounds straightforward enough on paper, in practice all its moving parts, not merely fuel, are backed by solid frontier technologies such as the internet of things

(IoT)—essentially the extension of internet connectivity into physical objects like trucks to collect and use data for analysis of metrics like truck location, driver behavior, etc., to optimize operations and ensure that a trip happens without a glitch.

Consider the following:

A journey between Delhi and Bengaluru requires Rivigo to allocate eight drivers over two full days who will coordinate with one another over eight pitstops where they need to do the handovers and get on to another vehicle in the opposite direction. This necessitates a tremendously precise degree of coordination in routing as there are drivers travelling in either direction at the same time. All of this activity is controlled through technology, i.e., a driver-friendly application that is more image- and less text-based and available in over ten languages. Through this application, a driver gets a 'duty alert', asking him to go to the pitstop. Here, he needs to scan his unique QR code before beginning his trip. Similarly, when doing a handover, another alert is received giving details of the driver to whom the truck must be entrusted.[7]

But beyond the seamless changeovers, Rivigo also has complete control and visibility over its trucks' movement in order to optimize wait times, track driver location and performance. In order to monitor all these factors, Rivigo's trucks are fitted with sensors and tracking devices.

"We capture 2,000 data points for every second through the course of the entire journey," says Kalra, explaining how data intelligence—facts and statistics, trends and aberrations—are mined for reference or analysis by the company to bring about improvements in decision-making based on past records.

For instance, better drivers or warehouse personnel are

allocated to handle fragile shipments based on past data in order to reduce accidents. Algorithms also take care of pilot rosters using data generated by the tracking devices to analyze for instance pilot location, number of hours he has put in and other factors before assigning journeys. IoT-enabled smart sensors meanwhile monitor trucks in real time to reduce breakdowns or control vehicle temperatures by studying data patterns to gauge the asset's condition, and taking timely action.

This has been critical for Rivigo to expand its full stack offering, which now includes cold chain logistics (temperature-controlled trucks to deliver perishable goods) alongside full-load express delivery and part-load services. Clients are directly able to make temperature adjustments remotely using an application, bringing in great efficiencies.

Rivigo is putting the huge trail of data generated from all these activities in predictive analysis of demand and pricing. "I can predict sitting here which client will give an order on which date so that we can have supply planned accordingly," says Kalra, illustrating how the company derives valuable insights from its huge repository of data.[8]

Much of this is unprecedented in the logistics sector in India. And technology is "evolving by the day," says Garg whose quest is to constantly push the boundaries and remain at the very cutting edge.

At the vanguard of this effort to transform the antiquated logistics industry is Rivigo Labs, the company's in-house technology think-tank, comprising possibly some of the best data scientists and industry 4.0 talent India has. Rivigo Labs has already filed patents in the US for its proprietary technologies that optimize fuel efficiency and pilferage, improve driver productivity and minimize in-transit damage of loads.

Patents have also been filed for matching drivers to routes based on geo-location which allow Rivigo to quickly map a driver closest to the location from where a delivery order has been booked, and put him on the job, or re-route another driver in close vicinity if necessary, by monitoring in real time the movement of its vehicles.

"Most companies have a reactive approach to technology. For Rivigo, it's proactive," says Deepak Gaur, managing director of SAIF Partners.[9] This tech-agility comes from Rivigo's carefully-devised strategy to keenly track the external environment and align its internal strategy accordingly.

> In a scenario of constant disruption, reworking short-term strategy to remain aligned with the dynamic external environment is absolutely important even when there is a 10–15 year plan that anchors the company's long-term vision.

"Two or three years ago, I did not believe that we will need such high-quality AI talent in the company. But now I believe that getting AI talent is a very big necessity. Not just a few hundred, we may need a few thousand AI engineers to come and work at Rivigo in the next ten years to deploy all the artificial intelligence-based technologies that Rivigo is experimenting with, from big data, to analytics, sensors and other automation tools. This was never the plan few years back. But, it's high priority now," says Garg, explaining why in a scenario of constant disruption, reworking short-term strategy to remain aligned with the dynamic external environment is absolutely important even when there is a

10–15 year plan that anchors the company's long-term vision.

It is this dynamism that has prompted Rivigo to think long-term and scout for talent outside India. It has plans to build capabilities overseas by opening an office in the US and collaborating with the academia to have a captive hold over future hires in the sphere of AI.

That Matter of Culture

"But while the arch of destruction (or technology) is long, it always bends towards the arch of culture," declares Garg, saying that while technology can give a company a lot of edge, if the execution culture is not right, the edge will diminish and you will decay.

Rivigo's exceptional execution culture more than anything else has been the vital reason why it has been able to scale so quickly. A lot of founders focus on business strategy in the early days but do not pay equal attention to building a strong cultural code. But a few years down the line, they realize that they cannot just create an organizational culture one fine day. Rivigo did not make that mistake. It focused on building a distinct culture from day one.

This meant literally writing down core beliefs or leadership principles and at the risk of being prescriptive, ensuring that they were followed to the T. These principles, Garg says, are the fundamental tenets that govern everything Rivigo does, from talent reviews to business evaluation or even hiring.

For instance, one of the stipulated HR practices is to hire people that are better than oneself.

"It is a concept very few traditional organizations understand. Think about it. Would you rather be on a ship where you are the smartest one around? The deepest learning happens on the job through your peers. Our hiring process is geared to test for attitude and alignment to our Rivigo Leadership Principles. We over index on this. Skills can be acquired easily if one has the right attitude. And experience is overrated especially when you are going into unchartered territories," says Kalra. Rivigo currently has over 3,000 members of staff on its payroll excluding drivers.[10]

Another major precept includes being data-driven to the point of obsession. Rivigo believes that 'the only source of truth' is that everything must be measured through numbers and data. Across functions such as marketing and sales, or while making investment decisions, measuring performance and charting growth strategies, Rivigo relies expressly on hard data rather than intuition or subjective emotion to accurately measure and scale its objectives and results.

But remaining at the cutting edge of technological disruption requires encouraging a strong culture of transparency and creativity. It is Rivigo's stated policy to encourage a clash of ideas, and 'respectfully challenge' the decisions of teammates if someone has a better solution.

"The best teams are those where there is a push and pull amongst team mates. They push each other to stretch more, take on new challenges and deliver and don't let their personal egos come in the way," says Kalra. "They laugh, they fight, they fall, they cry, they build and they deliver as a team. They critique each other and they support each other. This is what winning teams do! Give them any target and they would deliver."[11]

At Rivigo, pace is critical to delivery, but "it does not come from hustle. It comes from focus, clarity and concentration," says Garg. This is why the company does not celebrate people working 100 hours a week, but those that work with a clarity of purpose.

Rivigo believes that being purpose-driven at a missionary level over the past four years has significantly differentiated it from the others. It has a very ambitious reason for existence which is to use relay at a massive scale in order to make logistics human. And in everything that the company does the founders ask themselves whether it is making the lives of their truckers and clients better.

"We keep ourselves accountable to this purpose and measure our success through this and only this," says Kalra.[12] Having a solid purpose is what will eventually also lead to great profitability and market capitalization the duo believe. They do not pay a great deal of attention to metrics like turnovers or celebrate valuation milestones, because there is full comprehension that these are just short-term distractions and the journey ahead is a very long one.

"This makes us very input-focused. We don't really pay heed to the output because we know that maximum real output will only come through after putting in years of high-quality inputs into our innovation," says Garg. "Our KPI metrics are focused towards what's important for a long journey. And so, we don't celebrate 100-meter sprints. We also don't hire sprinters; we hire marathoners who can conserve their energy for the long haul."

This long-gestation thinking is an important enabler of experimentation without fear, without the expectation of instant results. It's why Rivigo has an appetite for failure, and in fact the ability to celebrate what it calls 'good failures that bring in valuable learnings'. It is why the company rewards for 'potential' not 'performance'.

"Learning happens at the edge of your comfort zone,"

says Kalra. "All these elements of culture when working in tandem create a flywheel effect which can leapfrog your organization through many orbits of growth and change. Rivigo is building a very unique culture where heroes thrive."[13]

Some of these practices have no doubt evolved over the years, and been learnt the hard way. Rivigo has been in the news often for its 'pressure cooker' performance-oriented culture, leading to hasty exits by key staff over the years. But as the company is growing, the volatility is gradually subsiding.

Into the Next Orbit

In less than half a decade into its existence, Rivigo finds itself in a sweet spot. While Garg and Kalra have painstakingly prepared the ground for a smooth takeoff, the surround sound in logistics is pleasing as well, with a fast-moving business ecosystem providing the company strong tailwinds to soar.

Between 2014 and 2019 there has been a sea change in India's digital landscape with smartphones and data penetration seeing an exponential rise and online payments becoming commonplace. After an exasperating two-decade wait, the GST, India's biggest tax reform, is a reality, with a potential to dramatically transform logistics. GST has created a unified market, making seamless cross-border transit a reality for logistics companies who previously had to go through red tape and complex taxation. This is a significant step in easing the business environment.

Also a booming start-up ecosystem has made it easier to find good-quality technical talent that is willing to join disruptive new-age companies like Rivigo rather than set out to chase the usual industrial behemoths. And customer service expectations have gone up significantly due to the rise of e-commerce and more exposure to global service standards which few in the logistics business are poised to deliver on as well as Rivigo.

But given the extent of its ambitions—to bring the entire Indian trucking economy on a relay model and become the largest logistics player in India—it does seem like Garg and Kalra's work has only just begun. "Building the future needs one to take leaps of imagination," says Garg. He imagines an India connected on relay and believes that at least 20–30 percent of India's trucking commerce will be online in the next ten years, with everything from shipment booking to delivery, fueling, brokerage, resale and financing facilitated through smartphones.

This will require Rivigo to make considerable capital investments in technology build-up. Its asset-heavy ownership model and pin code expansion over the years has pushed its profitability down the road. But much of Rivigo's asset buying will conclude over the next few years, and it envisages that a lot of the funds it raises will now go into technology investments. In the coming year, the company also expects to breakeven in the relay business.

But the biggest question remains one of scalability. In the past four years, Garg and Kalra have successfully trudged their way up to the base camp. But can they really climb Everest? Having successfully built their own relay model and an active freight marketplace, can Rivigo now put the third piece of the puzzle in place and convince truck owners and drivers to come on to the relay network for relay-as-a-service?

While the journey thus far has been remarkable, the

company's critics believe that many of the problems that Rivigo set out to crack have only been conceptually successful thus far. For instance, while its stack of technological innovations has been able to resolve long-standing trucking issues like fuel pilferage, metrics key for profit maximization such as reducing turnaround time in the relay system need to improve further. Currently the company has been able to achieve good results only on high traffic routes such as Mumbai and Delhi.

Rivigo has also had only limited success in getting its warehouse staff to use the application for faster loading and unloading or for estimating demand and supply based on the movement of its 5,000 trucks. This is a reflection of how difficult it is to deploy technology in a sector where a large part of the workforce are not savvy users.

Surmounting these barriers through constant iterations will be crucial to achieving the vision of making logistics human at a scale never seen before, and to making this India's innovation for the globe. For if they can conquer the complex Indian marketplace, there is nothing stopping them from taking the world head-on.

Sutras to Creating, Sustaining and Scaling Innovation:
Business Insights from the Rivigo Journey

Rivigo is the youngest of the companies featured in this book but also the largest if measured from a valuation perspective. Having emerged on the scene from nowhere less than half a decade ago, it is today a hyper-growth start-up leading the digital revolution in logistics, with a mission anchored in making the business more human at the same time.

Rivigo has been solving the industry's most pressing challenges using first-principles thinking, really stripping down complex problems to their atomic level and deriving original technology-enabled solutions to solve them at a scale never attempted before. So, while most of its peers were bringing incremental technology ideas to the market, Rivigo dug deeper to unearth conceivably the most significant challenge the industry faced and then created an effective solution to the problem that changed the industry paradigm.

The company's carefully-crafted operational culture over the years shows a close correspondence with at least five of our seven overriding principles of innovation:

Organization	Gap in the Market, Market in the Gap?	Flexible Approach	Customer Centricity	Capital Consciousness	Hiring – Passion Over Pedigree	Culture of Innovation	Amplification of Vision
Rivigo	✓	✓	✓		✓	✓	

Gap in the Market, Market in the Gap: Post 2013, a lot of entrepreneurs wanted to tap the vast opportunity that Indian logistics offered. There were clear gaps visible at multiple levels waiting to be plugged. But few could successfully identify the most pronounced one of them. Rivigo did! How? It is important to ask this because several start-ups do feasibility studies or conduct primary/secondary research to determine whether an already existing product/solution can address a gap they seem to have found in another context. The Indian start-up space is full of ideas imported from elsewhere. But few do deep-dive ground-level studies and engage with a gap in the way Rivigo did. Doing so gave it focused insights which led to an original, optimal solution that was tailor-made for the Indian context.

The way the company went about creating a market for its never-before-tried solution is also noteworthy. Rivigo figured that in order to establish the relay model and get the market to accept its idea, it needed to first own its fleet and test the product extensively for a few years before its worth could be proved to the broader trucking universe. Garg and Kalra had to resist the urge to instantly launch the relay as a service for other fleet owners through a marketplace model. And that was a right decision. Most aggregation ideas fail to take off because in their haste to launch and scale quickly they fail to adequately study the market, understand the complexities and fine-tune the underlying service. Rivigo's carefully-calibrated approach of first launching the relay through an ownership model, then separately building a non-relay aggregation platform (the marketplace) and now gradually bringing in relay-as-a-service has been a prudent way to create a market in the gap that it wants to fill.

Flexible Approach: As a company underpinned by fast-moving technologies, everything that Rivigo does is rooted in its broader purpose to make logistics human at scale through the driver relay model. But the company continuously aligns its strategy to dynamic short-term realities and the changing external environment in order to remain agile.

It also has a codified set of governing principles, which inform the culture of the organization. But these are not written in stone. They continue to evolve as the company grows and reaches new milestones. For example, when Rivigo was launched one of the leadership principles asked employees to be 'biased for action', which basically meant that they had to achieve a certain target even if it required hustling their way through it. However, that was replaced with something else as the company scaled and required less of the activation energy a start-up needs in the early days.

Customer Centricity: While the central idea behind starting Rivigo was to improve the lives of drivers, the relay model has inherent benefits built into it for the customer in the form of reduced delivery time. However, over the years, Rivigo has made continuous proactive efforts and investments to improve customer experience, which is today its biggest USP in the market from a business acquisition perspective.

Not only does Rivigo offer speed and price advantage to its clients, its deployment of sophisticated technology such as sensors has dramatically altered the way customers load cargo, track shipments and check for fuel efficiency. Furthermore, Rivigo's sophisticated use of deep data intelligence is enabling the company to make constant value additions to their offering every few months, which is one of the critical reasons why it has been able to convince many clients to shift from the unorganized to the relay setup.

Hiring – Passion over Pedigree: The level of technical competence required for a coding engineer at Rivigo makes it difficult for the company to fully ignore pedigree. The barrier to entry for a job at Rivigo is high and a lot of its talent counts the globe's Ivy League technology institutions as their alma mater. Nonetheless, the company's distinctive hiring philosophy places a great deal of importance on 'potential' rather than 'skill' and 'aptitude' rather than 'experience'. Rivigo believes skills can be developed over time. What is more critical is a hire's potential to internalize the organization's governing principles. It believes that finding the right people with the right purpose makes all the difference and is of utmost importance to an organization's capacity to deal with future challenges.

Some of Rivigo's other unique hiring practices include:

Not hiring when in doubt because just like a great hire can take the organization years ahead, a wrong hire can give setbacks that can prove costly. Rivigo considers hiring a "'critical moment of truth' and unless the entire panel of people is convinced of a candidate's ability to raise the bar for the organization, he is not hired.

Making a conscious effort to free the interviewing process of intuition, gut feelings or conscious or unconscious biases. Even hiring decisions are data-backed.

Culture of Innovation: Rivigo's lofty culture of innovation is a consequence of both the way people are hired and of how they are allowed to grow in the organization. Rivigo says it treats employees not like employees but owners being prepared for leadership roles in the future. This is a way to unleash the entrepreneurial spirit in each of them. An organization is as innovative as the sum of its employees. And a critical practice that allows innovation to percolate down the ranks at Rivigo is its unique performance assessment framework.

The company does not believe in annual performance reviews but in creating a loop of 'continuous on-the-job feedback, development and review' that focuses not just on past performance but also on a person's continuous personal development in the company and considers how well he is positioned to perform in the future.

The organization is very 'input-focused' and so it does not matter very much while assessing someone that they have performed averagely in the past few months. If they are bringing the right inputs that could potentially result in great innovation in the future, that potential is taken into consideration while reviewing a performance. The belief at Rivigo is that it is important to reward both performance and potential but there is greater importance placed on potential as that is the true mark of preparedness for a future-looking organization.

This future-looking, long-view approach is what propels people at Rivigo to be bold, show initiative and take risks that yield innovative ideas for the organization.

References

1. "A roadside chat set me on my way for Rivigo moment: Deepak Garg, CEO, Rivigo," *The Economic Times*, December 20, 2017. https://economictimes.indiatimes.com/small-biz/start-ups/features/a-roadside-chat-set-me-on-my-way-for-rivigo-moment-deepak-garg-ceo-rivigo/articleshow/62143469.cms

2. "Can India's street-smart logistics start-ups scale the final frontier?" *Techcircle*, August 23, 2018. https://techcircle.vccircle.com/2018/08/23/can-india-s-street-smart-logistics-start-ups-scale-the-final-frontier

3. "How dreams of logistics start-ups turned to dust," *The Economic Times*, January 21, 2017. https://economictimes.indiatimes.com/small-biz/start-ups/how-dreams-of-logistics-start-ups-turned-to-dust/articleshow/56695456.cms

4. "Rivigo shows how a humane but tech-enabled logistics company can command a billion-dollar valuation," *Yourstory*, March 12, 2018. https://yourstory.com/2018/03/rivigo-billion-dollar-valuation-journey/

5. "You cannot solve what you don't understand," *Inc.*, May 9, 2013. https://www.inc.com/thebuildnetwork/you-cannot-solve-what-you-dont-understand.html

6. https://yourstory.com/2018/03/rivigo-billion-dollar-valuation-journey/

7. "How two Indian start-ups are using big data to get ahead—and stay there," *Quartz India*, May 7, 2018. https://qz.com/india/1251872/rivigo-and-oyo-two-indian-start-ups-are-using-big-data-to-get-ahead-and-stay-there/

8. "Relay trucking drives in," *Fortune India*, January 15, 2018. https://www.fortuneindia.com/technology/relay-trucking-drives-in/101452

9. "Rivigo: Doing things that have never been done before," *Linkedin*, February 19, 2018. https://www.linkedin.com/pulse/rivigo-doing-things-have-never-been-done-before-gazal-kalra

10. "Rivigo: Doing things that have never been done before," *Linkedin*, February 19, 2018. https://www.linkedin.com/pulse/rivigo-doing-things-have-never-been-done-before-gazal-kalra

11. "Can Internet of Things disrupt the traditional trucking industry?" *HBS Digital Initiative*, November 18, 2016. https://rctom.hbs.org/submission/rivigo-can-internet-of-things-disrupt-the-traditional-trucking-industry/

12. "What product managers need to learn from pioneers in the past," *Yourstory*, May 11, 2018. https://yourstory.com/2018/05/product-managers-need-learn-from-pioneers-past/

13. "No shoulder to cry on: the triumphs and trials of Deepak Garg's pressure-cooker culture at Rivigo," *ETPrime*, April 10, 2019. https://prime.economictimes.indiatimes.com/news/68803107/technology-and-start-ups/no-shoulder-to-cry-on-the-triumphs-and-trials-of-deepak-gargs-pressure-cooker-culture-at-rivigo

4

ISRO

Space Odysseys on a Shoestring

November 5, 2013. Thousands of people are glued to their television sets across the country. From the studios of the state broadcaster Doordarshan, a commentator, with palpable excitement in his voice, counts down to a historic moment over dramatic live footage. The country's first interplanetary orbiter mission to Mars, the 'Mangalyaan', is being launched into space. "Five, four, three, two, one… it's a lift off…," yells the commentator, as a smoky crimson light fills the lower surface of the screen. From it, a slender rocket blasts off into the clammy afternoon sky, charting a magical crescent trajectory.

At the Satish Dhawan Space Centre in Sriharikota, the barrier island off the coast of Bay of Bengal in Andhra Pradesh from where the Indian Space Research Organization (ISRO) has launched this unmanned probe, onlookers take time to recover from the strident, wonderful roar of the 350-ton Polar Satellite Launch Vehicle (PSLV). Then they break into a rapturous applause. There are hugs, backslaps and high-fives.

Across the state, at the mission control room in Bengaluru, grave-looking scientists with furrowed brows and itchy fingers shift their gazes from the giant computer monitors feeding streams of data, and break into a smile. The first part of what is conceivably their most daunting task since India's space program began in 1962 has been successfully accomplished. There is a sense of relief. And the man beaming from ear to ear is Koppillil Radhakrishnan, chairman of ISRO, under whose guard this high-profile mission is underway.

'Mangalyaan' ('Mangala' meaning Mars and 'Yaan' meaning craft or vehicle in Sanskrit) marks India's first venture into the interplanetary space, and is a momentous landmark for ISRO.

It is an audacious start amidst the cyclonic season and has had to be postponed by a week as a result of technical issues. But things have finally gone off smoothly.

'Mangalyaan' ('Mangala' meaning Mars and 'Yaan' meaning craft or vehicle in Sanskrit) marks India's first venture into the interplanetary space, and is a momentous landmark for ISRO. While primarily a technology demonstrator mission, it also seeks to address some of the biggest scientific questions about the red planet, such as how Mars lost a bulk of its atmosphere billions of years ago and whether the climate there was once conducive to life.[1]

After 'Chandrayaan-1' when the country sent a lunar orbiter to the moon in 2008, undertaking a magnificent deep space endeavor such as this would help ISRO make further strides in answering profound questions about the universe such as the possibility of water on Mars, while also cementing India's position as a space power to reckon with.

Fast forward to ten months later and the scent of success looms large. On September 24, 2014, merely two days after the arrival of NASA's Mars Atmosphere and Volatile Evolution (MAVEN) Orbiter on the red planet, the Indian spacecraft enters the Martian orbit. In laymen terms, this entails leaving earth (the official beginning of space is 100 km above the earth's surface) and gathering enough force to break away from the gravitational pulls of the sun and the earth to enter the Martian orbit. In technical terms, it involves conducting six orbit-raising maneuvers and performing a crucial trans-Mars injection by lifting itself out of earth's gravity through what has been termed the "mother of all slingshots". After several complex trajectory corrections that requires precise calculations, a remarkable odyssey of 680 million km is completed.

"History has been created," beams prime minister Narendra Modi, as he takes the mic at the ISRO headquarters to address the country, wearing a sharp red sleeveless jacket. "We have dared to reach out into the unknown and have achieved the near impossible."

It is a 20-minute speech in which the country's powerful leader, who has sat in rapt attention at the mission control room, urges the nation to celebrate the power and mysteries of science. He echoes the sentiments of Manmohan Singh, the former prime minister under whose approval the probe was envisaged in 2012.

In May 2017, the Mars Orbiter Mission or MOM has

completed 1,000 days circling around the red planet, well beyond its designed 180-day life. It has explored and observed the features of the Martian surface, its morphology, minerals and atmosphere, with a specific mandate to search for methane in order to study the possibility or the past existence of life on the planet. It has relayed back over 700 images and continues to remain in good health, defying cynics who doubted the relevance and capability of this controversial probe.

The mission's astonishing success shines the spotlight on the decades of intense hard work and a high-performance organizational culture of innovation that ISRO has built through successive governments and leaderships. It shows how far the space organization has come in its own glorious journey since 1962, completing 90 spacecraft and 60 launch missions, sending over 180 satellites to space from 23 countries and boasting an impressive success rate of 94 percent.

'Mangalyaan' is truly the organization's crowning glory.

'Mangalyaan'—A Budget Sojourn

There are more than a few reasons why 'Mangalyaan' goes down in the annals of history as an extraordinary achievement. For starters, it gave India some serious bragging rights on the international stage, making it the first nation to enter the Martian orbit in its maiden attempt and also the first Asian country to do so. While missions from the US, Europe and the Soviet Union had successfully achieved this before, none had managed the feat on their very first go. Of the 51 probes sent to the red planet by then, 30 including highly publicized ones from China and

Japan had either malfunctioned or failed.

Not only was it a spectacular demonstration of India's soaring technological capabilities in the field of space science, but more than anything else, for a country dissed for its obsession with *jugaad* or a crass lateral-fix culture, it also set a fresh paradigm for frugal innovation.

Consider some of these statistics: the mission cost India $74 million, a number that is a mere fraction of the $670 million NASA splurged on its sprawling MAVEN probe. This made it the cheapest interplanetary mission in the world costing a mere ₹4 for every Indian. In fact, what ISRO spent on 'Mangalyaan' was $25 million less than what Hollywood put into making a single film, the space odyssey *Gravity* starring Sandra Bullock and George Clooney.

While the size, scope and complexity of missions vary significantly, there is no dispute that ISRO did accomplish the mission at an impossibly low cost. In fact, the agency claims that its satellites and launch vehicles as a whole are at least 50 percent cheaper than those produced by their western counterparts, and 'Mangalyaan' was no exception.

How did ISRO manage to attain this cost advantage?

It was through an exemplary four-step approach to project development that is common practice across all its space programs.

First, it used home-grown materials such as maraging steel, aluminum alloys, composites, chemicals, coatings and other high-temperature items to produce its own components wherever possible instead of using foreign imports. The goal was to reduce dependency on imported parts across critical systems and drive down costs. Today ISRO's import content has reduced from around 32 percent to 8 percent.[2]

This has been achieved by designing in-house and

intensifying collaborations with local manufacturers which also helped improve the local industry's engineering capabilities and technical know-how. This is something that can now be leveraged as the global space race hits a breakneck pace.

Second, this dependence on the local also allowed ISRO to work with Indian technicians who were paid less than half of what their counterparts in the developed countries earned, giving it a further labor-cost benefit.

Third, ISRO took a well-calibrated decision to build the spacecraft with the same structure and systems as 'Chandrayaan-1'. It used launch technologies that had proved their reliability in the past and modified and built upon them rather than starting from scratch. This modular, standardized approach significantly reduced new development costs. Engines and avionics common to different rockets and satellites were also optimally utilized to make this happen. Pre-launch testing was done with a view to minimize the number of tests but maximize their impact.

Finally, outside industrial capacity was leveraged wherever needed in order to avoid building new infrastructure in-house. This, ISRO realized, would be prohibitively expensive and unnecessary given the industry's competencies in developing complementary systems. In fact, ISRO is now intensifying its collaboration with the industry by opening its doors to the private sector to make not just components but full satellites rather than fabricating them in-house.[3]

The organization's cost-conscious approach was critical to carrying out an exercise like 'Mangalyaan' in a country like India, whose space priorities are often held to exacting scrutiny given the more immediate nature of our developmental problems and the fact that the country's entire space budget is funded by taxpayer money. But such well-calibrated cost planning has consistently allowed ISRO to keep India's space program, including missions like MOM, not only affordable but amongst the most cost-effective in the world.

A Technological Leap

Beyond proving to the world that it could cut costs without compromising on superior design and performance, 'Mangalyaan' also displayed the giant technological leaps India had taken in its space program.

The mission was carried out using a lighter launch vehicle, the PSLV. And even though its scientific objectives may have been curtailed as a result of this and other budgetary and technical constraints that prevented ISRO from launching a heavier satellite, 'Mangalyaan' demonstrated to skeptics from the developed world who had little faith in India's ability to successfully launch in such a short window that they were wrong.

From G. Madhavan Nair, the former head of ISRO, who had told *Science Magazine* that the mission "would be a national waste", and D. Raghunandan, secretary of the Delhi Science Forum, who called it "a highly suboptimal mission", there was no scarcity of skepticism regarding India's abilities prior to the launch.[4]

What then gave ISRO the confidence and capability to pull off this tremendous exploit with so much panache and against such odds? After all, the country was two decades behind the US and the Soviet Union in its space chase.

The answer to this lies not only in the scientific ingenuity and expertise of Indian scientists, but also in the calculated, incremental approach ISRO took to program planning and development under the skillful leadership of Koppillil Radhakrishnan.

Soon after occupying the C-Suite, Radhakrishnan expedited the appointment of an advisor to study the feasibility of the mission. He also commissioned a report that would delineate the complexities of such an undertaking, and was insistent that the attempt be made at the earliest available opportunity.

"Earth and Mars, based on their orbital geometry, come closer to each other in every 26 months so we had to capitalise at the earliest possible opportunity. If we missed this, we would have to wait for the next opportunity," says Radhakrishnan, explaining why the launch had to happen within a short span of 15 months.[5]

As the head of the mission, he realized that he had to galvanize his teams quickly to surmount several administrative and technological challenges, from providing augmented shielding to the spacecraft for harsh thermal and radiation conditions to building a reliable propulsion system that would work after a massive 300-day voyage.[6]

Most importantly, the mission involved tiding over fundamental constraints of capacity. The initial plan was to use the bigger Geosynchronous Satellite Launch Vehicle (GSLV) but due to various technical reasons, this would have delayed the probe by five more years. The trade-off then was between using a bigger, more powerful rocket and a speedier launch. Radhakrishnan and his team decided that speed was of the essence and took a well-calibrated decision to work towards ensuring that the narrow window of opportunity that ISRO had for the launch would not be missed.

In what showed an ability to make quick decisions and

lead from the front, Radhakrishnan deployed the less powerful PSLV launcher for the mission. The payload mass was brought down, making the probe lighter than what was ideal with relatively simple instrumentation on board. While this reduced the scope of scientific study, ISRO was clear that 'Mangalyaan' would not merely be a vanity project. Despite its size, it sought to address some critical questions regarding methane in the Martian atmosphere. It attempted to find out if methane-producing bugs or methanogens exist on the red planet—a relevant research topic at the time that dovetailed nicely with the ambitions of other more complicated missions carried out by the US and European agencies.

> ISRO's wisdom lay in understanding its limitations—time, money and capability—and with these in mind setting itself a complex but achievable target backed by a solid actionable plan.

ISRO's wisdom lay in understanding its limitations—time, money and capability—and with these in mind setting itself a complex but achievable target backed by a solid actionable plan that they could execute rather than fretting over an impossibly ambitious goal that was destined to fail. This brought about tangible results quickly, and also infinitely enhanced its capacity to creatively solve problems that arose as a result of the constraints put by a smaller probe.

"We… used our workhorse launch vehicle PSLV, with minimum modifications. We kept the expensive ground test to small number, while extracting best out of each test," says Radhakrishnan.[7]

Using the PSLV rocket required a novel approach to reach the Earth-Mars transfer trajectory. Because it was a lightweight carrier, it did not have sufficient power to place MOM on a direct course to Mars. As a result, the flight sequence had to be tweaked by first launching it into earth's orbit and then undertaking several maneuvers, before imparting additional velocity for entry into the Martian orbit. Necessity, as they say, breeds invention, and ISRO had to draft a one-of-its-kind technical plan that was tricky to maneuver, and required complex navigation strategies that tested the mettle of its scientists.

The team's resilience was also put to trial considerably during the months in which it was readying the PSLV for the launch. From the day the mission was announced by the then prime minister Manmohan Singh on August 15, 2012, to the day of the launch, ISRO had a thin execution timeline of 15 months. This meant being "schedule-driven to the extreme".

What it also meant was that unlike in Europe where scientists work 35 hours per week, ISRO scientists had to clock in 18–20-hour days.

Radhakrishnan was extremely cognizant of the fact that he had been given categorical support by the government despite ISRO's failure to develop the GSLV which could put heavy 2,000-kg-plus satellites into a high orbit and was far more suited for the mission. It was incumbent upon him thus to be as efficient as possible with 'Mangalyaan'. The challenge before him was to inspire his team of scientists by convincing them that they were part of history, of something larger than themselves. He also had to make them fully aware of the tight schedule that had to be followed even at the cost of putting their personal lives aside for a while.

Space science is all about teamwork and a probe like

'Mangalyaan' required building a team of not just smart but hugely committed people. The mission was only possible because of the personal sacrifices of each of the scientists who burned the proverbial midnight oil to make it happen. And it is no wonder at all that they could accomplish what they did without the addition of a single extra new hire.

"Our scientists and engineers always strived for a schedule-driven approach, which prevented cost overruns. Being time-effective made us cost-effective," says Radhakrishnan.

The combination of deft leadership, a committed, hardworking team that thrived in a culture of innovation and absolute bureaucratic and state support was what ultimately made 'Mangalyaan' a big success. But the achievement cannot be seen in isolation. It has to be seen as a continuum of a remarkable journey to understand the cosmos that began some 60 years ago.

To understand MOM's success, we will have to first see how far ISRO has come, and for that we will have to rewind the clock.

A Brick-By-Brick Story

There is a grainy black-and-white image of a slight gentleman carrying a rocket cone and riding a bicycle towards the Thumba rocket launching station in Kerala. It is that of scientist CR Sathya, shot by the famous French photographer Henri Cartier-Bresson in the 1960s. Another vintage photograph from the ISRO archives shows the Ariane Passenger Payload Experiment (APPLE), an experimental communication satellite, being tested on a bullock cart in the 1980s.

The two pictures are an evocative reminder of how far

India's space program has really come in the last six decades and its very humble beginnings when it commenced in the year 1962.

The Indian National Committee for Space Research (INCOSPAR), which preceded ISRO's formation in 1969, was set up by the Government of India with Dr. Vikram Sarabhai at its helm. It was INCOSPAR that established the Thumba Equatorial Rocket Launching Station (TERLS) at Thiruvananthapuram in order to conduct upper atmospheric research. The very next year it launched its first French-designed sounding rocket.

In 1972, the Space Commission and the Department of Space (DOS) were set up and ISRO was brought under the aegis of the latter. By 1975, four years after Sarabhai's demise, ISRO sent its first Indian-built satellite Aryabhata into space. This was under the stewardship of Prof. Satish Dhawan who, over the course of the next decade, expanded the vision of his predecessor by collaborating with overseas partners to launch and then build satellites, and broaden the drivers of the space program from science to space applications in fields such as telecommunications, broadcasting, earth observation and remote sensing.

In April 1984, Rakesh Sharma famously became the first Indian to travel to space as a part of the joint Indo-Soviet space mission and around a decade later, in 1993, ISRO had achieved complete self-reliance in space applications, developing the PSLV, a cost-effective and reliable light weight launcher that would become its workhorse over the next 20 years. PSLV has been used on historic missions like 'Chandrayaan' in 2008 and 'Mangalyaan' in 2014.

Today ISRO has three launch vehicles—the PSLV, the GSLV, a heavy expendable launch system and the GSLV MKIII which is intended to be used as the spacecraft for crewed space missions among other things.

Described by many as 'the beast', it is capable of carrying loads of up to 4,000 kg into orbits 35,000 km above the earth's atmosphere and double that weight into lower ones. Its launch, though not as sensational and headline-grabbing as 'Mangalyaan', is considered a milestone as significant as the development of the PSLV in 1993. It makes India self-reliant to launch much heftier satellites and is the result of a 30-year struggle through which ISRO built the cryogenic engine capability (which has powered a lot of NASA's rockets from scratch) without any international support.

Over the past few years, the frequency and complexity of ISRO's missions has only increased. It set a world record in 2017 when it packed 104 satellites into a single mission and released them into their individual orbits within a span of 12 minutes ensuring that they did not collide. This enabled India to script history. It was an unprecedented show of ingenuity and called for extraordinary design capabilities.

It has been a momentous journey for this agency thus far, traversing and growing through international bans, a closed economy, rocky governments and exasperating bottlenecks. Radhakrishnan calls it a "step-by-step progression, in the appropriate sequence". Each chairman, he says, "has enriched and enlarged the vision of the previous one, so that excellence is a continuum at ISRO". The pace of activity, he admits, is often "delirious" but the environment is such that it unleashes forces that allow for innovation to happen almost uninterrupted.

Force Drivers of Innovation

So, what are the forces that impel ISRO to embrace research- and technology-driven innovation so emphatically? What is it that gives it the institutional capability to carry out complex missions time after time and emerge as an exception to the moribund, anachronous culture prevalent among most other Indian public sector undertakings? How does it sustain the passion for knowledge and ideas among its 16,000-strong army of employees decade after decade and give wings to the creative instincts of staff who dream the impossible?

There is something fundamentally different about its organizational culture. To understand what makes it a standout innovator, it will be crucial to get a sense of the ingredients that have allowed ISRO to scale its technological prowess to a level that enables it to carry out sophisticated missions like 'Mangalyaan'.

Radhakrishnan puts it down into three broad points—i) operating structure, ii) organizational processes and iii) institutional culture.

Structurally, the Indian space program has always been spearheaded by an individual who is concurrently the chairman of ISRO which is the executing arm, the secretary of the DOS which is the regulator that ensures governmental, parliamentary and public accountability, and also the chairman of the Space Commission which is the policymaking body. And this three-in-one chief directly reports only to one other individual, the prime minister.

"What this means is that you've got to press the accelerator, the clutch and the break, but make sure you don't do it at the same time," quips Radhakrishnan.

Though terribly demanding on the individual at the helm of affairs because of the conflicting goals of each role, this integrated leadership structure has been tremendously successful in making ISRO an agile organization. This is because it allows the agency to sidestep India's elephantine bureaucracy at the ministry level and gives it direct access to the most powerful individual in the country who is merely a call away when an important project like 'Mangalyaan' has to be greenlit. It thus allows ISRO to cut through red tape, a business nuisance that can really stifle the innovative instinct of an organization.

"Irrespective of the party or person in power, all the governments have always been fully supportive of ISRO's space ambitions right from the beginning," says Radhakrishnan, giving politicians across hues a rare nod of approval in allowing this structure to flourish.

But while support from the government continues to be unflinching owing to ISRO's structural design, it is the long-term institutional operating processes at the organizational level that helps it consistently sustain and expand its goals without interludes.

For example, chairman tenures at ISRO change every few years. The gestation period of its missions on the other hand are quite long, i.e., 10 years or more on average. In order for stability to be maintained between regime changes, ISRO has designed systems that keep in mind the reality that one regime will plan, another will execute and possibly yet another will realize the task. This is to ensure that every chairman's vision is realized adequately and not thwarted after his tenure comes to an end.

A great example of how this organizational continuity is maintained is seen in the ISRO tradition of inviting former chairmen and scientists to continue and actively contribute to the mission development process post retirement. This gives leaders the ability to seamlessly expand on the vision of their predecessors and provides ISRO access to the most brilliant and trusted minds in the country.

"It lets us benefit from both the wisdom of the previous generations, and the power of the youth," says Radhakrishnan. New leaders almost form a '*guru-shishya* relationship' with the earlier leadership. And the fact that at least five generations of chairmen were present during the launch of 'Mangalyaan' in 2014 proves how strong these associations can be.

Beyond preserving the stability of the vision and containing potential corrosion due to leadership gaps, processes have also been adopted to optimize speed and capacity—the two other key ingredients that allow innovative ideas to thrive.

At ISRO, the staff are made to work simultaneously on several missions with differing timelines. Preparations on a future mission begin even before an upcoming launch is concluded. This 'lock chain' or parallel working strategy explains why its frequency of missions has substantially increased over the years.

The agency has also made it a point to learn from the setbacks it faced a few years ago when ventures like the first GSLV launch failed, causing long program delays. Since then, ISRO has begun making launch dates almost sacrosanct, giving no one but the management council the right to change them.

Achieving success in high-profile missions like 'Mangalyaan' and 'Chandrayaan' also requires a stable supply of the right talent which is the primary ingredient to success in this field. So, in 2007, ISRO decided to set up the Indian Institute of Space Science and Technology (IIST), backward-integrating its talent requirements by giving itself a ready catchment of new graduates. ISRO faced severe obstacles in hiring good-quality graduates who had begun to migrate to the more competitive software sector in the early 2000s, and this has helped it arrest that problem. It has also realigned remuneration and incentive structures to lure more people to join, and both these decisions have been vital to sustaining its ability to attract enterprising new hires.

All of these structures and processes have a direct bearing on the organization's ability to remain at the cutting edge. But it is the concerted effort in championing a unique culture of innovation in the organization that inspires its employees to continually strive for excellence.

The Culture Code

"The most powerful weapon on earth is the human soul on fire," said Ferdinand Foch, the French military theorist. Passion is an emotion that runs in the blood of all great inventors and ISRO naturally puts a premium on it.

"When you join ISRO, you give your 'I' to it," says Radhakrishnan.

What this means in actuality is not just a great emphasis on quality in recruitment, training and development of its human resources, but the ability of the leadership to drive among the staff, a much deeper sense of commitment and dedication to the job than a normal corporate scenario would require.

Communicating a sense of 'greater purpose' among its employees is fundamental to ISRO's success. It gives them the edge required to carry through with the radically unusual nature of the work they do, the hours they often have to clock in and the pressures they must withstand from the risk of failure or sharp media scrutiny.

But keeping staff inspired over a long career stretch is easier said than done, and one of the ways in which ISRO has managed to do it is by breaking down the boundaries at work. There is no room for hierarchy at India's space agency when it comes to technical, knowledge-based decision-making. A qualified junior person can chair a meeting, is empowered to voice an opinion that might be contradictory to that of his senior, provide constructive criticism and essentially have a voice to contest the pecking order if required.

> Keeping staff inspired over a long career stretch is easier said than done, and one of the ways in which ISRO has managed to do it is by breaking down the boundaries at work.

Breaking boundaries also means breaking internal silos. ISRO encourages open reviews where a system/product designed by one team is sent to be peer-reviewed by another. This creates an enabling and empowering environment of transparency, opens blind spots, brings more objectivity to the table and inevitably drives more productivity and innovation.

Giving employees the autonomy and freedom to operate comes with building an enormous appetite for failure though.

"We encourage failure, and we also encourage our employees to be transparent," says Radhakrishnan. "Fear, for instance, of being fired for a mistake, can dissuade them from reporting a small glitch or error they've made, but that can be catastrophic in the larger scheme of things. To avoid this, we give them the confidence to speak up."

Building and launching rockets is a multi-dimensional task that involves literally a few thousand people working simultaneously on the various components of the job. It is no surprise then that at ISRO the belief in the collective is very strong and credit for any mission is shared by the entire team.

"In the event of a failure though, the leader solely takes the blame, which requires a certain attitudinal mindset to prevail among the leadership," explains Radhakrishnan.

Launching New Dreams

What is next then, for India's space agency? Resting on its laurels is evidently neither an organizational trait nor an option, given how much more there is to achieve. For a space organization, 50 years is perhaps akin to adolescence and ISRO finds itself at the crossroads today. It has made great technological progress, and has over these years served an array of practical needs from natural disaster forecasting to computer communication, and its scale-up aspirations are expectedly loftier with a desire to improve the scientific utility of its missions.

It has plans to double the frequency of launches and conduct a host of high-profile missions in the years to come. It has already successfully tested a SpaceX-like reusable launch vehicle demonstrator and is working intensively to develop this vehicle re-entry technology which allows for recovery of all or part of the system for later reuse, further shrinking launch costs and stepping closer to space transportation.

By 2021–22, 'Mangalyaan 2', consisting possibly of an orbiter, a lander and a rover, will also be prepared for launch. Unlike Orbiters which only fly around the planet, Landers actually land and perform more complex experiments and analysis. A demonstrator-manned space flight to the moon is also in the pipeline, and if that is successful India will become the fourth country after Russia, the US and China to have successfully conducted a human space flight program.

The pipeline also consists of a mission to the sun, 'Aditya-L1', with a scientific aim to study unresolved questions in solar physics, as well as a potential orbiter mission to Venus.

The strides ISRO has been making in answering profound questions about the universe by undertaking these magnificent deep space endeavors has no doubt cemented India's position as a major space power to reckon with.

But while pushing the frontiers in technology ISRO remains acutely cognizant of the fact that its space program must essentially remain 'people-centric' and focused upon providing tangible benefits to the country from a developmental context, through communication, navigation, remote sensing, security and surveillance and other applications. And the systems built by it for application in some of these areas have no doubt been recognized as world-class.

The agency has however had to repeat ad nauseam to critics that only seven–eight percent of its total budget is spent on space exploration missions like 'Mangalyaan' that do not have a direct bearing on improving the lives of citizens. These too are undoubtedly tied to the broader developmental objective of finding applications for the common man.

But fighting this battle of perceptions may be the least of its worries going forward. Despite its impressive achievements, ISRO faces several challenges to retaining its exalted position in an increasingly competitive international space regime.

Critics have called for an all-encompassing policy framework to confront the various hurdles that could put the brakes on ISRO's ambitions to remain relevant in the global space race. This includes improving private sector participation (beyond component/parts supply), augmenting its launch frequency, meeting growing demands, realigning the focus of the space program beyond scientific and developmental goals towards military functions, retaining its position as a premier small satellite launch provider amid a flurry of new low-cost private entrants and optimizing its commercial potential.

So, in this unprecedented period of transition, with the space domain at an inflection point both commercially and technologically, is ISRO (and Antrix, its business subsidiary) correctly positioned to take advantage of all the opportunities that come its way?

"Without a doubt," says Radhakrishnan emphatically!

But between balancing its developmental motivations, taking brave but expensive moon shots and optimizing its huge commercial potential, ISRO is probably going to need a greater degree of boldness moving forward.

If its past successes are any indicator of what it can accomplish in the future, there is no reason to doubt that greater glory awaits India on its forthcoming odysseys into space.

Sutras to Creating, Sustaining and Scaling Innovation:
Business Insights from the ISRO Journey

ISRO has delivered at a level that few other government agencies have since its inception. The growing scale of the space agency's ambition is reflected through its many remarkable achievements: self-reliance in access to space with its own launch vehicles, significant use of space technology to demonstrate both technological capability and social utility, and strategic utilization of space assets as an instrument of geopolitics and foreign policy. ISRO has also developed a strong USP as the low-cost small satellite launcher of choice, commercially inking several contracts globally every year and running the most cost-effective space program in the world.

All of this has been possible despite having its back firmly against the wall and functioning in an environment riddled with constraints of ownership, finance, access to technology, international sanctions and public criticism. Embracing in its journey at least four out of the following seven principles of innovation delineated by us, ISRO holds several business lessons worthy of emulation despite its unique organizational structure and nature of work.

Organiza-tion	Gap in the Market, Market in the Gap?	Flexible Approach	Customer Centricity	Capital Con-scious-ness	Hiring – Passion over Pedigree	Culture of Innova-tion	Amplifi-cation of Vision
ISRO			✓	✓		✓	✓

Customer Centricity: People often misunderstand the purpose behind a poor country spending millions of dollars annually on space expeditions. ISRO has had a tough time explaining to critics that under 10 percent of its budget is spent on technology demonstrator missions like 'Mangalyaan'. The primary aim of the space agency has remained carrying out expeditions that are people-focused. Since September, 2015 for instance, it has been executing over 125 projects in collaboration with various departments across six areas including natural resources management, planning, monitoring and decision-making and disaster risk reduction.

ISRO uses data from communication, navigation and remote sensing satellites for a variety of purposes, such as for farming (crop damage assessment, crop yield estimation, crop production forecasting, etc.), water management, disaster assessment, monitoring of mining activity, sending automated warnings at unmanned railway crossings and weather alert messages to fishermen at sea. At the core of its operations has always been the customer (citizens), but these are not initiatives that make headlines despite scientists arguing that early Indian satellites were what paved the way for advanced disaster management systems and modern telecom infrastructure.

Capital Consciousness: The space race is an expensive one, and financing it is always a challenge in a developing economy constrained for finances. But ISRO has turned this adversity into an advantage by playing to India's biggest strength, i.e., *jugaad* or frugal innovation. Its approach to frugal innovation rests on four pillars—import substitution, standardized, modular designs that allow for the reuse of existing technological infrastructure and reduce new development expenses, cheaper labor costs and utilization of complementary industrial capacity.

ISRO's philosophy of aiming for lofty goals on a shoestring is a great lesson for entrepreneurs—don't let lack of money get in the way of dreaming high and striving for excellence. You can always do more with less if you improvise, optimize and reprocess!

Culture of Innovation: ISRO has an in-house guide of sorts that it has continually used in order to create a strong culture of innovation within the organization. This has been institutionalized within the DNA of the organization, and is not impacted very much by the changes in leadership. There are four major mantras that it abides by in order to filter this culture through the organization:

- **Ignite passions, rally staff around a "common greater purpose":** It is the only way you will get them to give it their 200 percent. Start-up founders have an important lesson to learn from here. Make your employees, who are working way harder than they would in a corporate job and taking a leap of faith with their belief in your idea, feel like important stakeholders.

- **Collapse the hierarchy! Tech nerds need a flat structure for creative juices to flow:** At ISRO it is not difficult to find youngsters critiquing someone much senior to them. At the operational level technical staff are fully empowered to execute their ideas and lead projects irrespective of seniority. At a more macro, structural level too, the absence of layers of bureaucracy that are present in any government body along with direct accountability only to the prime minister's office has unshackled ISRO in a way that cannot be underemphasized.

- **Break internal silos:** This is done by encouraging open reviews between teams to make processes transparent and strengthen ideas before they go out into the world. Outsiders or other teams, ISRO believes, are often better equipped to give objective feedback because they do not have a direct stake in the project, and can assess a situation or an idea dispassionately.

- **Give the freedom to operate and the freedom to fail:** Failure is encouraged at ISRO, but employees are asked to report it quickly, because hiding a wrong can often result in a bigger upheaval in the future. The organization does not believe in punitive action.

Amplification of Vision: Although ISRO owes its birth to the vision of Vikram Sarabhai, every subsequent chairman after him has built upon it and taken the legacy forward to harness the latest technologies in space science. Good leadership is critical to executing a strong vision and ISRO has put in practices to ensure that there is never a leadership vacuum at the top that will put continuous progress on hold. In fact, scientists and technocrats have always been the most important people involved in the decision-making, and ISRO makes it a point to hire leaders from within so that new chairmen maintain a continuum in project execution.

Continuity and innovation may seem like objectives at odds with one another, but in large organizations like ISRO which undertake intense, long-gestation projects, it is critical for leaders to concomitantly maintain a steadiness of vision and practice, while also creating a culture that supports transformative ideas. It is a tough balancing act that ISRO has been successfully doing for a long time. In fact, some former chairmen continue to actively contribute post retirement to see through the projects they have started. These management practices have been very important in ensuring that there is a quest for constant expansion of the agency's goals and ambitions.

Beyond these four principles, ISRO also holds up examples of other unique operational practices that have been valuable growth drivers for the agency.

There is no time like the present: Richard Branson famously said, "successful entrepreneurs don't wait for a perfect moment—they create it". Perfection is an elusive goal, and rather than falling into the all-or-nothing trap, ISRO has always chosen to work with what it had, rather than what was ideal. So, for example, there was no doubt that MOM had a smaller payload, and lacked the boldness of the missions conducted by other countries in terms of the scientific complexity of the payload but the agency repositioned it as a 'technology demonstration' exercise, rather than a science mission and used it as a stepping stone in its incremental capacity building and enhancement process. This is why it could do in four years what others took a decade to accomplish.

ISRO may not have acquired tremendous scientific value through the exercise, but it was a significant innovation milestone nonetheless for a variety of reasons:

1. It reaffirmed India's cost advantage and capacity to fabricate a light spacecraft entirely on home ground.

2. It proved the country's ability to see through complex maneuvers under severe budget constraints.

3. It incrementally enhanced ISRO's innovation capacity, preparing it for a bigger probe a few years down the line.

4. It put the country in direct contention with global superpowers as a worthy rival to watch out for.

Share the credit but not the blame. That is what good managers are supposed to do, but too many corporate scandals have shown us in the recent past that this is increasingly a rare leadership attribute. ISRO's leadership however has displayed time and again, in full public glare, that this practice—of taking responsibility for any failure, but sharing the credit of a successful launch with the entire team— is followed conscientiously by all its leaders.

President Abdul Kalam had famously narrated an example of this remarkable tradition at an event in Gwalior in 2006. When the SLV-3 mission could not achieve its objectives, Prof. Satish Dhawan took him in front of the press and said that he took full responsibility for the failure even though president Abdul Kalam was the project director. However, when the SLV-3 was later successfully launched again, Dhawan made him a key stakeholder in the success story of the launch in the press.

What could be a more effective way of motivating employees to excel?

It would be difficult for many in India to believe that a public sector undertaking could offer lessons in business excellence. ISRO, we can agree, contradicts that notion many times over.

References

1. "Why India's Mars mission is so cheap – and thrilling," BBC, September 24, 2014. https://www.bbc.com/news/science-environment-29341850

2. "Isro's Mangalyaan triumph has silenced Mars critics," *Firstpost*, September 25, 2014. https://www.firstpost.com/india/isros-mangalyaan-triumph-has-silenced-mars-critics-1727623.html

3. "ISRO awaits advanced materials," *The Hindu*, August 22, 2018. https://www.thehindu.com/sci-tech/science/isro-awaits-advanced-materials/article24754393.ece

4. "ISRO's century emboldens it to embrace private sector!" *The Economic Times*, July 3, 2016. https://economictimes. indiatimes.com/news/science/isros-century-emboldens-it-to-embrace-private-sector/articleshow/53028494. cms?from=mdr

5. "K Radhakrishnan interview: Success due to tireless efforts of Isro," *Hindustan Times*, September 24, 2014. https:// www.hindustantimes.com/india/k-radhakrishnan-interview-success-due-to-tireless-efforts-of-isro/story-Uz4BU6xpPeU8kHmTUamBlO.html

6. "K Radhakrishnan interview: Success due to tireless efforts of Isro."

7. "K Radhakrishnan interview: Success due to tireless efforts of Isro."

5

Forus Health

Democratizing Eye Care through Cutting-Edge Technology

Early in September 2016, as the ten-day Hindu festival of Ganesh Chaturthi commenced in Mumbai, a long line of devotees queued up in front of a technician with a compact, portable eye-testing device outside the crowded Siddhivinayak Temple.

For seven days, around the clock, some 13,000 people who came in to offer prayers to Lord Ganesha, got their eyes checked on their way out of the shrine. It took precisely a couple of minutes for each one to get screened and figure out if there was anything wrong with their vision. By the end of it, 14 percent or more than 1,800 of the 13,000 people that were tested were detected with abnormalities and given a 'Need to See a Doctor' report.

The machine generating this analysis in this non-medical setting was '3nethra classic'—a portable, non-invasive, non-mydriatic imaging device that is revolutionizing eye screening in India. It was invented by Forus Health, a remarkable Bengaluru-based social innovation enterprise, which was founded by former Philips India employees K. Chandrasekhar and Dr. Shyam Vasudeva Rao.

Since its inception in 2010, the company has made it its singular mission to prevent avoidable blindness, using cutting-edge technology to detect eye ailments quickly and cheaply.

India currently has around 12 million blind people out of 39 million globally according to a report published by the National Programme for Control of Blindness (NPCB) in 2017 titled 'Definition of blindness under National Programme for Control of Blindness: Do we need to revise it?' That is a whopping one-third of the world's blind population. For a developing country with limited healthcare infrastructure, this is a colossal socio-economic challenge, and for the individuals and their families, an emotional and social setback that lasts a lifetime.

The irony is that 80 percent of this blindness is preventable. But the skewed ratio of ophthalmologists to patients in India—there are barely 20,000 eye specialists for a population of over 1.3 billion people—makes it virtually impossible to detect and treat common eye problems on time. The shortage of doctors is compounded by several other issues like low patient literacy and paying capacity, the lack of medical infrastructure, particularly in rural areas, and a mindset that is not attuned to preventive screening.

Forus Health has cracked the code to overcoming all of these barriers through its ingenious range of 3nethra screening devices that are advanced, affordable and accessible.

In less than ten years since it began operations, the company has captured a significant market share in the ophthalmological imaging space in India. It has built a presence in 34 countries across the world, installing over

2,400 devices. To date, 3.5 million individuals have been screened and 600,000 people have been saved from losing their vision as the compact, affordable devices cost roughly a quarter of what competitors charge. The company, which is on the cusp of turning profitable, has raised two rounds of venture funding and over $13 million from marquee investors such as IDG Ventures, Accel Partners and Asian Health Funds. It has also filed 21 patents.

Having disrupted the retinal imaging market, Forus Health now manufactures not only the flagship 'classic', but also numerous other value-added next-generation products to screen premature babies and treat other more advanced eye ailments. Through these cutting-edge innovations, it is targeting one goal, i.e., to shine some light on the entirely avoidable darkness that fills the lives of millions of blind people.

This is a true-blue indigenous manufacturing success story, that has been driven by local innovation but which has also quickly caught the advanced world's attention. It is a double bottom-line company that has combined profit with a grand purpose, a fact that promises to keep the brand relevant for several years to come.

Midlife Muse

Forus Health was born out of inspiration that came at a time when its two founders were settling into the humdrum of midlife professional accomplishment. K. Chandrasekhar, an alumnus of the Indian Institute of Management, Calcutta (IIMC) and the Birla Institute of Technology and Science (BITS Pilani), was Director of Strategy at NXP Semiconductors, a division of Philips India while Dr. Shyam Vasudeva Rao, who earned his doctorate from the Indian

Institute of Science (IISc), was Director, Technology, at Philips Healthcare. Both men were at the peaks of their respective careers and neither had plans to disrupt their comfortable lives of business-class travel, five-star-hotel stays and other perks.

But a chance meeting in 2005 with Dr. S. Aravind from the Aravind Eye Hospital, at a session arranged by Philips for its senior managers, pretty much changed their lives. Chandrasekhar and Rao sat in rapt attention as Dr. Aravind elucidated his company's much-renowned infinite model for healthcare, and the dream he had to cure the world of blindness through a unique business philosophy that allowed it to treat millions across the globe for free or at a subsidized rate while still remaining profitable. It was the first time that the duo got a sense of the pervasive problem of preventable blindness and its magnitude in the country.

> Forus Health was born out of inspiration that came at a time when its two founders were settling into the humdrum of midlife professional accomplishment.

Aravind was (and continues to be) the largest provider of ophthalmological services in the world, addressing this issue through low-cost surgical procedures, standardized care, performance management, high staff productivity and rigorous cost control. But the talk triggered Chandrasekhar's and Rao's minds in another direction. It got them to think about how they could look at the issue through the lens of technology. Since a bulk of the cases could be avoided through early detection, they wondered if technology could be leveraged for better preventive rather than curative care.

Their association with Aravind began initially through Philips as part of small corporate social responsibility (CSR) projects where they would help the latter set up human resources (HR) processes or devise strategy. This was not part of their key responsibility area (KRA). They had to do it on their own initiative over and above their other core responsibilities to their organizations. But soon, the project began taking up most of Chandrasekhar's and Rao's spare time.

By mid-2006, Philips decided to discontinue its association with Aravind due to a non-alignment with their core business but the duo continued to help in their personal capacity, often dedicating evenings and weekends to formulating management strategies or programs to improve Aravind's efficiency and productivity metrics.

"Through the course of these interactions, we really began getting intimately connected with the problem of preventable blindness and developed a behavioral understanding of why things were the way they were," explains Chandrasekhar.

Understanding the Challenge

So, why were things the way they were?

Why, despite the availability of multiple medical technologies, were there so many blind people in India? Why had the global multinational companies (MNCs) working on ophthalmologic care not been able to fill the very big gap that clearly existed in preventing cataract, glaucoma, diabetic retinopathy, cornea and refractive errors—basic eye ailments that were the cause of 90 percent of blindness cases? These were some of the questions that

Chandrasekhar and Rao grappled with as they got deeper and deeper into the problem.

Lack of early detection and screening, they found, was undeniably the big culprit. But being engineers with a keen eye for design, the duo gradually came to recognize that the devices that were available in the Indian market for screening eye disorders were primarily to blame for the situation.

These were, by and large, imported products which were completely designed to suit the needs, health systems, price points and challenges of customers in the West. They did not consider the ground realities of the Indian landscape which was riddled with its own peculiarities and that prevented mass screenings from taking place.

For one, the vision care system in the country was plagued by an abysmally-low doctor-patient ratio, i.e., 1:65,000. Unlike in the West where an ecosystem of paramedics or optometrists examined basic eye defects, the burden of screening in India was largely on this very small population of doctors.

These practitioners were constrained by the cost of the diagnostic devices which were a prohibitively expensive investment for most of them to make. Moreover, in order to diagnose different eye diseases investments in different types of devices were required.

Furthermore, the MNC-designed systems were a complex combination of optics and electronics. As a result, they were massive in size and required trained staff and hospital infrastructure to be operational. They were not easily portable.

The grossly underserved rural market, where eye care infrastructure or doctor availability were often lacking, could not thus be penetrated with any ease.

Also, most fundus cameras used in these devices needed drops to dilate the eye in order to obtain a better view during screening. This was a time-consuming process that discouraged people from going for regular check-ups because in a poor country with a large population of daily breadwinners, time was literally money.

The challenges were clearly well-defined while the existing product offerings were not addressing them. They were unaffordable, bulky, complex to operate and simply not designed keeping the local market's idiosyncrasies in mind. The issue required, what Chandrasekhar calls, a "paradigm shift in thinking" that focused on a solution that would radically address the design flaws to democratize the screening process.

The Three-A Principle

Clearly, what was needed was a dimensional change and it became increasingly clear to Chandrasekhar that it would have to come in the form of a disruptive new 'made for India' product that would take into consideration the local needs and milieu.

The existing set of manufacturers had a commercial approach to the issue of blindness in India. Their motive was purely profit-driven and not focused on eradicating the disability or getting a large population to have preventive check-ups done. They simply wanted to sell to the 15,000 ophthalmologists practising in the country back then, at the highest possible margin and were, as a result, pushing ready products created for different contexts into the market rather than making something that was optimally aligned to the specific Indian need.

Chandrasekhar understood that for the problem to be addressed effectively, he needed to take a diametrically opposite approach, i.e., focus on creating a product that could get around the limitations of the system (lack of adequate eye doctors being one) using technology that could be deployed at scale, through minimally-trained technicians or the larger ecosystem of 500,000 general physicians (GPs) in the country. This would expand the delivery of eye healthcare at an exponential rate. The avenues of screening and the number of people doing them had to be significantly increased.

> The existing set of manufacturers had a commercial approach to the issue of blindness in India. Their motive was purely profit-driven.

"Our mission," explains Chandrasekhar, "became solving the problem of preventable blindness. The development of 3nethra was a consequence of this, not of simply wanting to develop a medical device and profiteer from it, which is the approach our competitors had taken."

And so, in 2009, equipped with a problem statement and a gamut of complex insights, Chandrasekhar put in his papers at Philips and decided to start out on his own. Dr. Rao would join him a few years later.

It was a risky, bold decision. Chandrasekhar had two young school-going children and the usual familial responsibilities that would have deterred many in his position. But he was driven by an inexplicable urge to conquer the absolutely avoidable crisis. He was also a spiritual man, and a trip around this time to the pilgrimage site of Kedarnath in Uttarakhand cemented his resolve to go ahead with his plans. There his inner voice told him to follow his heart.

The general belief in the medical devices industry at the time was that replication of another manufacturer's product could address problems of proprietary innovation. More than 90 percent of what was available in the market as a result were reverse-engineered varieties of existing devices. But Forus Health did not have either the option or the inclination to do this. The existing products were simply not intended to address the large gaps in the market and so copying would simply not work.

"So, we thought we would develop something by thinking like GE and Philips when it came to product design and innovation, but have the heart of a philanthropist, so as to serve a larger population," says Chandrasekhar.

It was this unique frame of reference that made Chandrasekhar recognize that he needed three As—**accessibility, affordability and advanced technology**—built into the solution he designed. It was the only way in which preventable blindness could be eradicated at scale in an environment where the existing technology was too expensive, bulky and complicated for mass screenings.

3nethra: Built for Scale

With various concepts playing around in his head, it was time to take the leap from idea to execution. The first thing that Chandrasekhar did after he quit was look for funding so that he could start on the prototyping process. Having understood the problem deeply, he did not have trouble communicating his vision effectively and managed to raise a round of angel money worth ₹1.5 crores, impressing an individual investor with his depth of management expertise and the value proposition of the idea he was seeking to actualize.

Chandrasekhar himself was a hardware engineer with a solid background in the semiconductor industry. He hired a small office space and a few engineers to write the software code, outsourcing the optics part to a company in the Netherlands. Some experts from the IISc were also roped in to collaborate on the development of the product.

It was a gruelling year and a half of trial and error, spent incorporating all kinds of market inputs and feedback into the design, and also included testing and validations from ophthalmologists. Finally, the first prototype was released in January 2010 with Aravind Eye Care being the first company to receive it.

"It was a simple, non-bulky head-mounted display, with cameras that picked up retinal images that fit all the specs. But when we took it to Aravind they said no one will take the product seriously, because it didn't look like a traditional ophthalmological device that they saw being operated in the movies, or even around them," recalls Chandrasekhar. "Their feedback was that if you want the customer to believe in the authenticity of the product, try meeting their existing perceptions of how it should look."

Since the end objective was to convince as many people as possible to get themselves screened and take the end output seriously enough to want to go to a doctor for treatment, the team went back to the drawing board, spending another year fine-tuning their product.

By 2011, the first '3nethra classic' was finally launched into the market, having gone through a series of tests and design evaluations. Aravind Eye Care became its first customer, and leveraging the iconic brand's credentials in the market allowed Forus Health to promote the product credibly among other individual ophthalmologists and hospital chains.

The product was the result of remarkable engineering ingenuity and frugal innovation. But most critically, it was an outcome of having paid close attention to the market's precise needs and demands.

The need was for something that used technology advanced enough to produce images which could detect a problem, but also affordable and accessible to a wider population of technicians who did not necessarily belong to the small community of ophthalmologists, so that it could penetrate deeper and get more screenings done.

And 3nethra ticked all the boxes!

From a design perspective, it took care of the **affordability** aspect by bringing the cost down to just about ₹5 lakhs whereas the rate for most other non-mydriatic devices was ₹18–20 lakhs. How was this done? Most device-makers used lenses made by global companies such as Zeiss and Cannon for their cameras. These specifications were essential for advanced diagnostics, but not for screenings. So, Forus Health got rid of all the add-ons such as additional lenses and filters, and only retained optics that were good enough to indicate the early onset of an ailment.

3nethra also had more bang for the buck because it was a five-in-one device. It could detect five ailments that caused the majority of the blindness cases in India, thus eliminating the need for doctors to buy more than one device. Also, because it was portable, one device could be shared among many doctors or health centers.

The **accessibility** barrier was broken in a couple of crucial ways. First, the size of the product was reduced so that it could fit into a suitcase and become portable. Second, unlike other devices, it did not hardwire computers into the cameras which added to the bulk and made them immobile. Instead, 3nethra was embedded with a cloud-based telemedicine feature, a very new technology at the time, that facilitated remote diagnosis in places outside a hospital environment such as health camps and even at the doorstep of a patient. From here, 'Normal' or 'Need to See a Doctor' instructions generated by automatic screening algorithms could be sent back to hospitals or clinics for further advice from the doctors. Finally, the device was designed in such a manner that it could be easily assembled and used by even a non-technical, minimally-trained operator, circumventing what was perhaps the biggest challenge to overcoming the problem, i.e., the lack of adequate numbers of doctors.

The **advanced technology** that facilitated these design elements was supplemented with other pragmatic features such as minimal electricity requirements to operate the device. 3nethra used only 10 watts of power and ran for four hours on an uninterruptible power source (UPS) which made it optimal for rural screenings. Forus Health designed the optics to capture the image of the retina without the need to dilate the eye, quickening the screening process which encouraged more people to get themselves tested.

Keeping Sharp Focus

There is much to learn from Forus Health's early days for product start-ups looking to scale up.

Few companies climb the ladder purely on the strength of their product design. But Forus Health is a rare exception. 3nethra's design was built for scale. Everything about it, i.e., the pricing, the business model and the features were driven to reach a maximum number of people rather than profit from a few.

> The strategy—of playing a volumes-game by appealing to the market of 500,000 general physicians, optometrists and paramedics through a cheaper, smaller, rugged, less complex product—paid off.

It was a consequence not just of incredible engineering capability, which Chandrasekhar and Rao ensured by hiring the finest talent they could get hold of, but also of acutely studying customer insights and incorporating the minutest feedback into apposite product development.

The company had to radically alter its mindset in order to arrive at this level of design resourcefulness, and take counterintuitive decisions like downsizing product attributes and reducing costs when others were differentiating themselves through value addition and more advanced features.

"Our very ambitious vision, which was to eradicate blindness, prevented us from looking at the problem as a 300–400-unit market, the way others like TOPCON or Zeiss did. We always wanted to expand the scope of screening beyond the ophthalmological ecosystem, and eradicate potential blindness among millions," says Chandrasekhar. "We did not want to restrict ourselves to the standard places where someone would go for an eye examination. We had a larger purpose and knew that when you address a large problem, economies of scale are not just built in, they are assured."

The strategy—of playing a volumes-game by appealing to the market of 500,000 general physicians, optometrists and paramedics through a cheaper, smaller, rugged, less complex product—paid off, allowing Forus Health to expand the reach of ophthalmological devices beyond eye doctors and target a much bigger market segment that was by and large ignored by the industry.

Apart from the design and pricing, it was also the decision to integrate the internet module for remote diagnostics that served as a key differentiator for the company, allowing it to quickly scale through urban centers and penetrate the deep hinterland.

Despite the positioning and pricing advantage though, market acceptance was the biggest challenge in the early years. The eye devices market in India was controlled by big Japanese, European and American names, with not a single local player in the ophthalmic imaging space. So, despite being targeted at the mass screening market, convincing the broader ecosystem to trust a local start-up proved to be challenging.

As a result, Forus Health made a conscious decision to begin deployment from the top of the pecking order, selling initially to specialist ophthalmologists across chain hospitals like Aravind Eye Care and others, so as to build credibility and get a vote of confidence from the broader community. The decision worked in their favor. Within three years it had the distinction of having undertaken the largest fundus camera installation in India, something that made people sit up and take notice.

To put things into context, Chandrasekhar 'outsold' what his competitors had done in sales terms in a decade, twice over and in half that time.

Beyond the Classic

For companies that pride themselves for being innovative, however, product development is not a one-off move but a continuous process. They incorporate customer reviews to improve subsequent editions, and continuous feature enhancements are undertaken to advance the value proposition and meet dynamic and changing requirements. As the flagship product gathers prominence, it becomes critical also for founders to look at ways and means to do related diversification and build a portfolio of offerings. For this, it is important to put together a project management and research and development (R&D) function that simultaneously works on the future pipeline.

Chandrasekhar followed this course quite earnestly, continually investing in research to roll out newer products even as '3nethra classic' was being sold in the market with a great degree of success.

This explains why the company has been so prolific in increasing its range of offerings in such a short span.

In under two years since the launch of '3nethra classic' in 2011, Forus Health unveiled '3nethra royal', which was an improved version of the former, equipped with an objective refractometer function and a more advanced telemedicine module integrated into it. This was followed by the launch of 'flora' in 2015, a diagnostic device that took detailed images by carrying out a process called fluorescein angiography.

Then a year later, in 2016, after three years of a 40-member team working on R&D, and a 6-month-long pilot project, it launched '3nethra neo', a game-changing wide-field imaging system that screened babies for retinopathy of prematurity, a condition that can result in permanent blindness among premature infants if not detected early on.

There were no devices readily available in the market to treat this disease which was caused during the neonatal intensive care of premature babies. The excess oxygen supplied by the incubators has an adverse effect resulting in retinal detachment. This potentially affects 3.5 million babies. The '3nethra neo' was a market disruptor because there was only one device available for neonatal retinal imaging, but it was ridiculously expensive, costing $140,000 and above.

Chandrasekhar's team adopted a standardized modular approach to product line expansion whereby smaller parts or independently-created modules were duplicated rather than recreated for each new device. This is what made their process so quick, cost-effective and imminently scalable.

The company also made a determined bid to cast its net wider and wider with every passing year, studying the ecosystem to uncover areas of intervention that would allow it to expand quickly and touch as many lives as possible. This is reflected in its new line of devices in the refraction or vision correction space such as the '3nethra Specto', a next-generation digital phoropter that is soon to be launched. The 'Specto' can do subjective refraction without physically changing lenses, which is a great aid for giving prescriptions for spectacles even in remote lenses. It has also launched the 'Aberro', a hand-held refractometer that uses next-generation wave front technology to take accurate refractive measurements for patients from 5 to 80 years.

According to Chandrasekhar, refraction is the biggest problem in the world with 125 million people visually impaired due to uncorrected refractive errors. The number of people who require vision correction globally is 4.6 billion, out of which only 2.1 billion have already got it corrected. The other 2.5 billion have not and a simple reason for that is the lack of access to an optical shop.

"They need to be reached differently. Through school screening, home screening, subjective refraction and through quick prescriptions," says Chandrasekhar. "Our devices are focused on that." The 'Specto' for instance gives the operator the ability to email, text and print a patient's eyeglass prescription in real time. The average examination time meanwhile is just 10–15 seconds.

With the launch of these devices today, the company's footprint and commitment to preventing blindness has grown exponentially from the time its operations began. "We are now calling ourselves a technology company for vision management," says Chandrasekhar as he gradually begins to build a presence across various related sub-segments of the eye care market.

Going Global

Along with expanding its product portfolio and growing its reach in India, a substantial scale-up in Forus Health's operations also happened from a geographical standpoint.

Today 3nethra installations have crossed 34 countries, with the company getting its products registered by the Food and Drug Administration (FDA) in the United States (US), so as to expand in the developed world. It has also built a high-profile team in the US to grow operations and take advantage of the massive potential the global market offers, given that blindness is a worldwide issue.

Chandrasekhar believes that there are three important reasons behind the phenomenal success it has achieved globally.

1. 3nethra products were built from scratch, and were not, as has been explained earlier, reverse-engineered varieties of something that already existed. As a result, the company was able to file patents, and pass internet protocol (IP) diligence tests with flying colors. It is absolutely critical, says Chandrasekhar, for product start-ups to build an intellectual property portfolio that does not infringe upon other technologies because it makes expansion into international markets much easier.

2. From a marketing standpoint, Forus Health kept the product positioning dynamic. So, "A tool for eradicating blindness in India, became a convenience screening device in the US," says Chandrasekhar. The mantra was: differentiated marketing to grow in different geographies.

3. Finally, there were continuous enhancements made to the device; it was customized as far as possible for different needs. For instance, in Africa, the '3nethra classic' works on solar lighting as electricity is a massive issue. "As an innovator you cannot sit in an air-conditioned space and design in a vacuum. You have to go to the remotest places and take care of all practicalities and deliver a product which meets the conditions on the ground," says Chandrasekhar, reiterating what has been a constant motto at Forus Health.

From kiosks in commercial buildings in Mexico to community programs in Guatemala, eye clinics in the Philippines, outreach camps in Zanzibar and doctors travelling on boats in the Amazon to reach remote tribes,

3nethra's acceptance across terrains is widespread today, an accomplishment not too many young Indian companies can boast of.

As of today, the company's global operations contribute to nearly a quarter of its sales revenues, but in the coming years it expects that pie to grow to 50 percent, given how uniquely positioned the company is to trim costs for the developed markets and minimize inefficiencies in the developing world.

A Platform for the Future

Much has changed in the ten years in which Forus Health has been in business. Individuals like Dr. Shyam Vasudeva Rao who were instrumental in the organization's growth have exited the company. But several new people have joined the mission which, despite the fruits of monetary success, steadfastly continues to prevent avoidable blindness.

In fact, with increased success Chandrasekhar's desire to expand Forus's influence in the eye care sector has only become more well-defined. 3nethra's wide adoption across the globe has inspired his resolve to widen the company's reach and go deeper into the problem. If in the first leg of the journey, the task was to take screening out of the shackles of ophthalmologists and open it up to a wider ecosystem of GPs, paramedics and optometrists, the dream today is to further democratize the whole process. Chandrasekhar hopes to take screenings to railway stations, airports and any other place where there is, as he describes it, "health-seeking behavior and an intention to pay for it."

In order to do this, the company has begun shifting focus from outright sales to a subscription model whereby its devices can be rented. This is a way to reach a wider ecosystem of people for whom the core business is not eye screening and who thus may not wish to invest ₹4–5 lakhs on a machine.

"Let's say you are someone who runs eye camps, or even a GP. You treat 50 patients a day, of whom ten are diabetic. I ask you to screen those patients because 30 percent of them are likely to have diabetic retinopathy. You won't have to buy my device. I will give it to you for free, but you will have to pay me a prepaid subscription of ₹10,000. For every patient you screen, I deduct ₹200. What you charge above that to the patient, is your margin," says Chandrasekhar, explaining how the subscription idea works.

Chandrasekhar hopes to take screenings to railway stations, airports and any other place where there is, as he describes it, "health-seeking behavior and an intention to pay for it."

This model is paving the way for Forus Health to gradually become a platform rather than remain only a device manufacturer. Since these subscriptions are connected to a network of ophthalmologists, optometrists and other stakeholders on one dashboard—a website or an application—similar to any other e-commerce website, the supply chain of eye care is connected end to end.

So, for instance, after a screening at the GP's clinic, the 'Normal' or 'Need to See a Doctor' report is instantly recorded on an application through the cloud, and the ophthalmologists on the platform can download these case files, see the images and prescribe treatment. In addition to devices, Forus Health has developed competencies in cloud and artificial intelligence solutions which are used to analyze photographs captured by 3nethra devices and can with high accuracy diagnose specific diseases.

"The platform approach will help us delve into many aspects of eye care, including hosting complementary devices or services not devised by us, but put on the market through our portal because they are essentially involved in solving the same problem as us," explains Chandrasekhar.

Chandrasekhar also wants to gradually expand this idea to vision care, whereby its hand-held refraction devices will be rented out to optical shops which in turn will be put on to the Forus Health platform and connected to customers keen to get their vision examined.

"So, if you are sitting at home, all you need to do is log on to the platform and put in a request for someone to come and do your eye examination at a stipulated time. The system will identify an optical store that rents our device nearest to you, and have the examination completed," explains Chandrasekhar, adding that it will empower the bricks-and-mortar stores, already losing business to online chain optometrists, while also improving patient convenience.

While these plans gradually take a more concrete shape, Chandrasekhar is setting ambitious targets for the company, hoping to increase the number of screenings from the current 2.5 million to 10 million people in the next two years. The new platform approach, he expects, will drive this exponential growth going forward.

Forus Health also has a range of new products and upgrades in the pipeline to pave its entry into the premium market in Europe and the US.

Having been a forceful market disruptor, the big challenge that Chandrasekhar believes he now has to plot a course through is professional jealousies and a backlash from the industry that had hardly expected an outside start-up to come in and conquer what was legitimately their territory. There are rumblings of that already and he can feel them. But his belief in his product and the support of a strong 120-member team makes him confident of being able to tide through difficulties on this front.

The bigger test really is keeping himself motivated and passionate about the cause after a decade in the business. The only way to do that he says is to tell himself that it is still an unfinished business and will be so until preventable blindness is fully eradicated from the world.

That is a long way off, but there is no denying that Forus Health is making significant headways to get there.

Sutras to Creating, Sustaining and Scaling Innovation:
Business Insights from Forus Health's Journey

Delivery of healthcare to the poor is often a nearly insurmountable challenge in India because it involves overcoming several barriers of capacity and technology. It calls for the coming together of different factors to achieve significant results. There are many moving parts to the healthcare delivery chain, and very often, they do not all work in tandem. This inevitably leads to failure.

Forus Health's remarkable achievement, which involved the capturing of a market larger than that of its competitors in ophthalmological imaging in under ten years and doing so by serving large numbers at the bottom of the pyramid, is the result of getting all these parts to move at once, solving multiple pain points with one simple, widely scalable solution. Its revolutionary product design has plugged the gaps of accessibility, affordability and advanced technology all at once, addressing several constraints posed by infrastructure, limited availability of doctors and state capacity.

This cutting-edge product design though is also backed by solid business practices and an adherence to at least four out of our seven principles of innovation.

Organization	Gap in the Market, Market in the Gap?	Flexible Approach	Customer Centricity	Capital Consciousness	Hiring – Passion over Pedigree	Culture of Innovation	Amplification of Vision
Forus Health	✓	✓	✓				✓

Gap in the Market, Market in the Gap: It was not as if there were no imaging devices in the market before Forus Health to screen patients for eye deformities. But Chandrasekhar's unremitting focus on 1) outlining his real goal, i.e., eradicating preventable blindness, and 2) defining the target market for his product, i.e., a much broader ecosystem than merely ophthalmologists allowed him to find a precise gap, and build a device that would go on to address the design flaws that his peers were overlooking in their products. It led him to develop something that was market-appropriate and would facilitate screenings at scale, democratizing the process significantly so that 80 percent of avoidable blindness cases could actually be prevented.

Chandrasekhar did not spot the design flaws instantly but instead had to engage with the problem of preventable blindness for years before these insights could be turned into actionable modules for the product. Along with a keen understanding of the flaws in his competitors' products, his motivation to solve the problem rather than merely profit from it, was critical in driving him towards an optimal solution. Chandrasekhar's approach, unlike that of his counterparts, was altruistic first and commercial later. He was purpose-driven, rather than profit-driven.

"Personally, I feel that ten or 20 years from now, every company will seem like a social enterprise, as you cannot move away from the society and do something. You have to have some social impact from what you are doing, and that's how you reach true scale," Chandrasekhar told Soum Paul, the author of *Flight of the Unicorns: Lessons from India's Start-up Bubble.*

It is interesting to consider how this altered, non-commercial gaze has helped him to achieve what others could not.

Chandrasekhar's MNC counterparts focused only on monetary rewards while deploying their products into the market, an approach that prevented them from investing their minds into crafting an idea that would bridge the social gap meaningfully. On the other hand, it was Chandrasekhar's larger societal purpose and his empathy for the cause that pushed him towards finding a solution that fit the precise market need. Social innovation requires this purpose-driven approach, as has been proven time and again.

American author Napoleon Hill once said, "The starting point of all achievement is desire. Keep this constantly in mind. Weak desire brings weak results, just as a small fire makes a small amount of heat."

Chandrasekhar's desire was not only big, it was right. As a result, his solution was more potent.

Deploying the solution or creating a market for it was the next challenge. It is extremely tough to change buying mindsets and push out established players, no matter how innovative or groundbreaking one's product is. Chandrasekhar was David dealing with MNC Goliaths who had tremendous industry networks and marketing prowess.

However, his trump card was the connection with Aravind Eye Care, which was in some sense made of the same flesh and moral fabric. And so, once they agreed to install his device, using that credential to sell to other chain hospitals or those at the lower end of the supply chain became easier. But while Forus Health did twice the sales of its competitors in half the number of years, Chandrasekhar does not yet believe that he has built enough of a market in the gap. Because unlike them, his target is to eradicate blindness, not merely increase the number of units sold.

Flexible Approach: Forus Health has continually displayed an ability to take customer feedback, both negative and positive, and use it to make tweaks and additions to its offerings. This flexibility is what has allowed it to grow so fast.

Right from promptly going back to the drawing board and changing the design of its head-mounted prototype after Aravind suggested they make it look more like a traditional ophthalmological device, to keenly absorbing market knowledge in order to make series-wise improvements to its products, there has been no rigidity on the part of Chandrasekhar to change and adapt.

While many product start-ups make the mistake

of resting their entire business on a single product, particularly if it is doing well, its flexibility in being able to change direction, or pivot as it learnt of new customer demands or market opportunities led Forus Health to constantly make delta improvements and even launch newer versions that addressed micro-markets like pediatric screening or related ailments like refraction, and introduce a subscription-based service model to expand reach.

It is an organization that has not remained static as a result of its flexibility.

Customer Centricity: This is a metric that is built into the very design of 3nethra. In fact, the device is a result of Chandrasekhar's absolute focus on patient behavior and circumstances, right down to the fact that it needed to be mydriatic because poor patients could not afford to waste time on an eye-screening exercise if it required the dilation of the eye and took very long, as that meant missing work which they would not do. It is such close attention to customer (patient) behavior that informed the design of 3nethra.

In fact, a fundamental difference between 3nethra and the other products in the market was that they were doctor-centric, not patient-centric. Democratizing eye screening however necessitated a shift in focus from doctors (who were very few in number to solve the problem) to patients by using technology that would bypass the constraints posed by limited medical expertise.

As it grows its presence globally, the company is mindful of the fact that customer circumstances will vary with geography and it takes care to customize the product as far as possible for different conditions. For instance, it has enabled the use of solar power to run the devices in Africa where electricity is an issue.

Amplification of Vision: Forus Health's leap from product to platform reflects the company's rising aspirations. It no longer just wants to remain a screening device manufacturer but, as Chandrasekhar describes it, morph into a "technology company for vision management" so that it can touch a huge number of lives and deliver services everywhere from state-of-the-art hospitals to railway stations and little vision kiosks in malls.

There are logical worries about how the shift from a sales- to a subscription-based rental model will impact core revenue streams, but Forus Health's primary goal is to expand its reach as much as possible. A research article published by Deloitte University Press in 2017 titled 'Turn Products into Product Platforms' shows that an effective product platform creates "significant economic value for third-party participants" thanks to network effects and also yields "strong returns for the platform builder" eventually.

In fact, according to Stern Strategy Group, a public relations and brand advisory firm, "Products deliver a single revenue stream, platforms generate many." The jury is out on whether Forus Health has the capability to execute its vision and build a strong network of ophthalmologists, optometrists, GPs and other vision management stakeholders on one platform, and create a supply chain of eye care that is connected end to end. If it does manage to do it, it will be a force to reckon with.

Forus Health's absolute obsession with integrating cutting-edge technology into its product line has thus far been a big reason behind the giant leaps it has taken in the last ten years. And today the market is providing the much-needed tailwind. According to the Associated Chambers of Commerce and Industry of India (ASSOCHAM), an information technology- (IT-) industry body, India's telemedicine market has been growing at the rate of 20 percent compound annual growth rate (CAGR) every year, and is expected to cross the $30 billion mark by 2020 as wireless technologies decentralize healthcare in India.

Being an early mover on these trends definitely gives Forus Health a distinct advantage to chart a future roadmap for accelerated growth.

6

Agastya International Foundation

Igniting India's Minds from the Bottom Up

It is 10 am on a Monday morning and the Government Higher Primary School (GHPS) in Bengaluru's Yelahanka suburb is in a hubbub of activity. An energetic bunch of kids with neatly combed hair and wearing chemical-blue uniforms engage in a steady hum of casual banter until the sight of a colorful minivan entering the campus impels some of them to disrupt the standard orderliness and leap out of class with visible excitement on their faces. Soon, the whole lot is on the ground, animatedly lining up to look at a curious array of scientific instruments, working models and experiential tools that an instructor pulls out of the van and lays out in the courtyard.

Over the next hour, a horde of smiling faces pour over plastic replicas of the human body, gaze with wonder at a model of the solar system and bombard the instructor with a volley of questions about a chemical reaction they have just witnessed, their faces lighting up every time he answers them with a live demonstration

This is the scene of an Agastya International Foundation mobile lab in action, one of the many held in schools such as GHPS Yelahanka across rural and urban India, in a bid to instill a sense of wonder and scientific inquiry in school children. Agastya does this by dispensing with the archaic 'chalk and talk' method of rote learning that students in India endure, exposing those from underprivileged backgrounds in government-run schools to fresh, experiential, real-life pedagogy. And the mobile vans are just one of the many ways in which Agastya is spearheading an educational revolution.

Agastya was founded in 1999 in Bengaluru by Ramji Raghavan, a high-flying ex-banker who abandoned a lucrative job with Citibank in New York to return to India. The organization was founded upon a rather unique, if not esoteric mission—to spark curiosity, nurture creativity and instill a sense of confidence in India's children and school teachers by using hands-on science as a medium!

In a country where the Annual State of Education Reports (ASER) reveal a monumental failing of the basic education system—50 percent of students cannot read books meant for kids three years younger to them, less than 60 percent can read time from an analog clock and under 20 percent are employable by the time they graduate—this seemed like a pipe dream to many at the time.

But in the 20 years since Ramji first dreamed up his lofty resolve in 1999, Agastya has made a significant dent in the country's education landscape, supplementing and complementing the onerous task the government has of harnessing India's massive demographic dividend. It has reached 12 million children through 250,000 teachers, 200 mobile vans, over 75 labs on bikes, 95 science centers and a sprawling 172-acre creativity campus that acts as the feeder laboratory for it to run what has become one of the largest hands-on science education programs for children and teachers in the world!

Evidence of the efficacy of Agastya's unique approach is perceptible while conversing with the kids at GHPS Yelahanka, their minds stirred and their behaviors often fundamentally altered due to the intervention.

Agastya was founded upon a rather unique, if not esoteric mission—to spark curiosity, nurture creativity and instill a sense of confidence in children and teachers by using hands-on science as a medium.

Inside the computer lab after the mobile van leaves for the day, little Nisha from the seventh standard relates how learning about electrical circuits made her force her parents to change the incandescent bulbs in her home and shift to LED. Abhishek from the eighth standard says that he no longer needs to mug up before exams but remembers all the concepts as he has performed the experiments with his own hands. Then there is 10-year-old Jayashree whose day identifying plants with an Agastya instructor for her botany lesson has inspired her to plant 50 saplings around her house. She says that she wants to become an environmentalist. Darshan's latest passion, he insists, is making compost for his neighbors by segregating waste. This he learnt during a video-based learning exercise that Agastya carried out.

These are deprived kids who often do not have a square meal to eat, but have had their minds ignited by Agastya. And it was precisely with this objective—to nurture an imaginative young population and build an inspired nation from ground up—that Ramji started his journey back in 1999.

Homeward-Bound

Ramji was born and raised in a family of high achievers—his father K. V. Raghavan retired as the chairman of Engineers India Ltd., and his maternal uncle Dr. P. K. Iyengar as the chairman of the Indian Atomic Energy Commission. It was a 'twist of fate', Ramji acknowledges, or an accident of birth, that separated him from the vast majority of his less fortunate countrymen who endured the indignity of poverty and disease as he strode ahead in life, building a successful career in high finance that took him trotting across the globe.

But his rural roots in an exclusive township in remote northeastern Bihar (now Jharkhand) and schooling at the famous Rishi Valley School, an alternative boarding institution run by the Krishnamurti Foundation of India in rural Andhra Pradesh, had made him acutely aware of his privileged circumstances and the need to do something to improve the lives of those around him.

And so, it came as no surprise to anyone when at the peak of his career, Ramji kicked a rewarding career that held the promise to take him even higher in the corporate hierarchy to return to his roots.

His formative years at Rishi Valley School where independent thought, creative freedom and a deep, intimate connect with nature were at the center of the learning process, had had a profound impact on him. He was also greatly influenced by Jiddu Krishnamurti's approach to education which was hinged upon encouraging a deep sense of inquiry within students at a very fundamental level. As a schoolboy, he had dreamt of living in mythical Shangri-La, a dream which matured into a desire to run a school in the foothills of the Himalayas which would nurture creative leaders. These persuasions coupled with his own passion for social justice and an intense feeling of discontent about his own line of work firmed up Ramji's resolve to come back.

It was clear that education was the field where he wanted to intervene. His own exposure to learning was in stark contrast to the largely uninspired, dictatorial pedagogy that was the norm in India, where the teaching environment often churned out dull, unimaginative students bereft of original ideas or a scientific temperament. And he was thirsting to pass some of what he had inherited.

But vague notions of dabbling in education were not enough. It was vital to articulate a powerful, distinctive mission, and upon his return, Ramji spent months polishing his own thoughts about how and where he should intervene. The coming together during this period of his father, uncle as well as several other advisors and luminaries with a wide range of expertise, such as S. Balasundaram, the ex-principal of Rishi Valley School, Mahavir Kumar, a Rishi Valley alumnus and the former president of the Bangalore Stock Exchange and Dr. R. Krishnan, a former DRDO scientist, helped him fortify an idea. This was of an education that was fun, practical and interactive and moved science away from conventional classroom-based rote learning.

"Don't copy anyone, do something that others would want to copy," was critical counsel that Dr. P. K. Iyengar, the famous nuclear physicist, gave him at this juncture. It was advice that really stuck in his head, making him think big and out of the box.

It had always befuddled Ramji that India, despite having a large, young and intelligent population, lagged behind other countries on several innovation indices and he could only see the largely uncreative educational system as the reason for blunting the instincts of students and preventing them from seeking anything more than a well-paying job.

He believed the status quo had to be altered by bringing about a fundamental shift in a child's attitude to learning from 1) 'yes' to 'why', 2) 'looking' to 'observing', 3) 'passiveness' to 'exploring', 4) getting him to use his hands to touch and feel things rather than read about them in a textbook and 5) replacing fear with confidence.

The Ah-aha-ha-ha Mantra

In essence stimulating the spirit of what he called-**Aha-ha-ha!**

Ah!—awakening a student's mind to abstract scientific concepts with simple, affordable models and experiments made using materials like coat hangers, balls of string, potatoes, etc. For example, most kids find it difficult to understand how electricity is generated. But Agastya conducts simple experiments to show this using potatoes. Here, metallic wires are inserted inside the potato so that they become electrodes by reacting with its sugar, water and acid contents, and illuminate a bulb. The first reaction of the kids when they see this is, ah!

Aha!—promoting a sense of inquiry and exploration and encouraging students to investigate the logic and reasoning behind what they have seen.

Ha-ha!—arriving at a state of delight after having conquered one's fear about a formless idea, thereby improving retention, performance and instilling a sense of confidence in the student.

"Very few people, if any, in India or around the world had voiced a mission like that," says Ramji. "And therein lay a big difference between what we wanted to do and what others were doing in the domain of education."

Kuppam—The Cradle

There were two strands that had to fall into place to execute the grand mission that Ramji and his close coterie of advisers had laid out.

First, they needed a space where ideas that would give Agastya the academic backup to inform its pedagogy would germinate, and second, train teachers who would then translate their vision into actuality in classrooms. Both had to be located in a single place, and hence a decision was made to acquire a large creativity campus modeled on the ecologically diverse Rishi Valley School.

This, they envisioned, would become the nodal hub of innovation with experiential model-making labs, cutting-edge computer facilities and other intellectual resources for curriculum building that would serve a catchment of schools in a particular district or state and over the years proliferate across the country.

Neither Ramji nor his core team had ever built anything from ground zero. They were all essentially service professionals. Translating their dream into a living, breathing reality however required money, a network of contacts and an ability to effectively communicate an idea that had no precedent.

Having articulated a mission, Ramji spent the next

one year readying the groundwork for Agastya's future. He rapidly expanded Agastya's sphere of influence, onboarding an array of erudite and well-respected advisors and trustees which included retired scientists, government administrators, academics, bankers, creativity trainers, designers, doctors, parents and life coaches.

These were people who were mostly outside the traditional turf of education but were passionately interested in making a difference. And each would bring to the fore best practices from their own turf. For example, the practical experiments to be used for teaching were designed by scientists from the Homi Bhabha National Institute, allowing Agastya to instantly benefit from the best possible pedagogic material available in India.

Onboarding these 'outsiders' was a deliberate, counterintuitive decision, because Ramji knew that those well-entrenched within the system would instantly dismiss what he was proposing as his own ideas were vastly different from the standardized mainstream models of learning followed in schools.

His goal—to inspire curiosity in students through real-time exposure to science—was ambitious and he needed people from the outside who were untarnished by pre-existing biases about how education must be imparted to help him in his quest.

His unusual idea to engage 'non-experts' from the field had three significant upshots that allowed Agastya to leapfrog instantly:

1. The cross-pollination of perspectives from a diverse set of people who were not beholden to or prejudiced by the existing system unleashed a volley of unusual but brilliant ideas that gave

Agastya new, invaluable insights to further develop the action plan for the creativity campus that was truly different.

2. He could leverage this influential network to gain access and present his idea to people in a decision-making capacity. For instance, then chief minister of Andhra Pradesh, N. Chandrababu Naidu, was instantly impressed with Ramji's out-of-the-box approach and sanctioned 172 acres of land at the prevailing market rate to set up the creativity campus. Land acquisition in India is a frightening pursuit that has often led even the most influential foreign investors to pack their bags and leave, so this was literally a lottery.

3. The sheer depth of expertise that the advisors brought along with them gave the project a credibility and heft that made seeding the venture easy.

Two US-based Indian entrepreneurs, Sandeep Tungare and Ravi Reddy, immediately pumped in $100,000 and another friend of Ramji's wrote a check large enough for him to buy the sprawling piece of land.

By April 2000, barely a year into Ramji's return, Agastya had not only crafted a unique mission and registered as a public charitable trust, but was also equipped with a large piece of land where Ramji could sow the seeds of his dream. It was no mean feat.

The land though was an undulating, rocky patch of barren wasteland in Gudivanka, a remote rural area in the Kuppam district bordering Karnataka, a far cry from the verdant Shangri-La of Ramji's dream. He was initially disappointed but his father's words of wisdom comforted him at the time.

"Don't look at how things are today, look at what they have the potential to become tomorrow," he had said, with the prescience of an astute futurist. These were words that were immensely valuable at the time.

A Speed Bump and a Change in Plans

It is often said that entrepreneurship cannot be taught, that it needs to be learnt—by falling and failing, by getting one's feet dirty, by feeling that first sting of insecurity. No matter how successful one may have been as a professional, it is no guarantee for a win at surviving the vagaries of private enterprise.

Ramji learnt this lesson early on in his journey. Clinching a prized piece of land and raising the funds to buy it was a big triumph, as was rallying a large set of accomplished advisers around him to help create the intellectual software for Agastya's training programs, which included designing the curriculum and experiments, planning effective interventions, staffing the labs, etc. And he expected his luck to persist.

But the land at Kuppam was remote and barely approachable, and resources which far exceeded Ramji's budget, had to be dedicated to building access towards it.

In about a year, Ramji's pockets ran dry and he had no money left to spend on the infrastructure—classrooms, innovation labs, ecology parks, personnel—essentials necessary to kick-start operations. He was under tremendous duress to deliver on his promise and justify the investment to his investors, the government and even the several trustees and advisors who had come on board.

He had been mistaken about the amount of money that was required to fulfil the scale of his ambitions and had overestimated his ability to raise funds for a non-profit venture.

No matter how successful one may have been as a professional, it is no guarantee for a win at surviving the vagaries of private enterprise.

"Having handled high-profile commercial and investment banking functions at gigantic Wall Street institutions, I was used to money coming through in a jiffy after a good internal presentation to the board. And I naively allowed myself to believe that the same would happen here too," admits Ramji. Some bit of overconfidence had also crept in given how easily he had managed to raise the initial round of seed funding. But little did he realize then that as a small social entrepreneur working in a non-profit set up, every subsequent fundraising exercise was going to be a hard sell. It was a setback that would considerably delay Agastya's plans, but would also become a massive learning curve for Ramji.

Most importantly though it proved to be a turning point for the fledgling organization in defining the very operating model that has given Agastya the true scale it has today, i.e., its mobile science labs.

A crisis often provides powerful impetus for disruption, and stuck in a desperate situation with no job or money and with his reputation on the line and his dreams in jeopardy, Ramji was frantically in search for answers. What could he do if he did not have basic infrastructure ready for children and teachers to come to him?

"Go to them?" suggested Mahavir Kumar, the managing trustee, during a car journey to Coimbatore. "If they can't come to us, we should go to them."

The casual remark turned out to be a moment of great revelation! An epiphany that helped Ramji realize that all that was really required to begin operations was a minivan and some teaching material that instructors could take from school to school. They did not really need to wait for a building to be erected to start work. As obvious as the solution may seem now, it had required a jolt of potential failure for this creative response to be elicited.

The team quickly got to work. Through Dr. PK Iyengar, who had joined Agastya as a founder trustee, Ramji immediately managed to get hold of a low-cost trunk of objects needed for science experiments, that the Homi Bhabha Centre for Science Education had developed. He also called a friend at Hindustan Motors and requested him to dispatch an old transport van. And soon enough, he had set the ball rolling with a mobile lab which was traversing the rural landscape of Karnataka and Andhra Pradesh to ignite young Indian minds. Balaram, the tractor driver at Kuppam, was trained to be the first mobile lab driver–instructor. The campus, Ramji convinced himself, would come up in due course.

The initial response to the mobile labs was tremendous. Entire villages began flocking to the vans to see the experiments that Balaram would carry out. Beyond imparting knowledge about the subject, Balaram encouraged children to ask questions, explore a topic using all their senses and used 3D models to make abstract textbook concepts more real. The curriculum was designed by collaborating with the best minds across academic institutions and the quest was to move the child's mind from 'wow' to why and to how.

The villagers were so unexposed to such visits that on one occasion in a tiny hamlet they even mistook the science demonstrations for trickery and tried to break the windshield of the mobile lab. But the Agastya team persevered through such challenges as they could see the results of their interventions almost instantly.

Within a few months, parents became more supportive of their children's education because they could see first-hand what their kids were learning by going to school. Class teachers reported improved levels of understanding among students as what they taught no longer remained theoretical concepts. The decision to go to the students had proved to be an instant success.

Fortuitously, in this period Ramji also met Alok Oberoi, a London-based private banker. Oberoi was completely roused by Ramji's story and his fresh thinking, and wrote him a check for $20,000. He also promised to commit a similar amount every year and it was his generosity that sustained Agastya's mobile van operations till 2003, the year in which Ramji met the man who truly became the wind beneath Agastya's wings.

A 'Rare' Encounter

A couple of years running the mobile labs had convinced Ramji and Mahavir Kumar that what they had going was a game changer. It was low-cost, asset-light, replicable across geographies and quickly scalable. And the staggering response their minor intervention had evinced further validated Ramji's belief that he was on the right track because, soon enough, the Government of Karnataka took note of Agastya's activities and asked him to put similar vans in operation all over the state. It was a big opportunity to scale. They wanted Agastya to also build science centers in urban and semi-urban areas where kids could take a day off from school and plunge into experiments.

The catch, however, was that they were willing to shell out only the operating costs while Agastya had to raise the capital required to fund the infrastructure.

Ramji also had not given up on his dream of a large central bricks-and-mortar operation at Kuppam where the grandeur of his vision could come alive through a biodiverse open-air ecology lab spreading across several acres, cutting-edge experiential zones where children could immerse themselves in science, and a space where he could hold intensive teacher-training workshops.

While the mobile labs acted as the spokes, a central hub, he felt, was still an essential node. He now envisioned it as a 'school for schools' or an ideas factory where through sustained R&D a knowledge base on new modes of teaching could be developed for implementation through the mobile vans.

All of this boiled down to just one thing—he needed to raise the money that matched the scale of his ambitions!

This was around 2003, and on a visit to Mumbai, a casual conversation with a banker friend, Pankaj Talwar, changed the course of Ramji's destiny. Talwar told him that he could think of no one in India who had the capacity to understand his vision better than a man called Rakesh Jhunjhunwala. He agreed to set up a meeting between the two and then one morning Ramji landed up at the office of Jhunjhunwala, a legendary billionaire, well-respected in the world of stock markets and often referred to as India's Warren Buffet for the terrific success he has had with his investments.

A large man with twinkling eyes, a lazy casual manner and an astuteness matched by few, Jhunjhunwala was known to be a keen judge of both the crusade and the crusader before he decided to put his money on the table.

He gave Ramji a patient hearing and was intrigued with his proposal. There were two things that convinced Jhunjhunwala to extend his support to Ramji:

1. He had not met many like him who had quit a rewarding high-profile career to dedicate his life to a higher purpose that did not yield many monetary benefits. That to him was evidence that Ramji meant business and could be trusted implicitly.

2. Ramji's unique quest to spark curiosity jumped out at him. Jhunjhunwala was himself a tremendously questioning child and he credited his success in life to honing this spirit of inquiry.

He agreed to fund one mobile lab but also told Ramji that he was not quite sure about the bricks-and-mortar campus idea.

Ramji though instinctively knew that he had found a benefactor who shared his passion for bringing change. A few months later, he went back to meet Jhunjhunwala again and convinced him to donate two more vans. Some more time elapsed after which Ramji told Jhunjhunwala that he had come to him not 'asking' but 'begging' for something more substantial because he wanted to build the first computer center at Kuppam.

His passion for the cause moved Jhunjhunwala who sent him away to get his father's blessings, and wrote a check of ₹20 lakhs for the first building—the Jhunjhunwala Centre—to come up at Kuppam.

Over the next couple of years, Jhunjhunwala must have keenly observed Ramji's progress because one afternoon in 2006, he casually asked Ramji to drop by his office. Sitting alongside him was Manish Gupta, an ex-BCG executive and numbers man. Jhunjhunwala asked Ramji what was new and Ramji told him that he was just back from a visit to Frank Oppenheimer's Exploratorium in San Francisco and was thoroughly impressed with the 'library of experiments' concept where students could explore scientific phenomenon and improve their ability to understand the world around them. He wanted to do something similar at Kuppam and needed more money.

The Government of Karnataka took note of Agastya's activities and wanted them to build science centers in urban and semi-urban areas where kids could take a day off from school and plunge into experiments.

Jhunjhunwala agreed to fund Agastya's Exploratorium (later renamed Discovery Center). It was at this point that he told Ramji there was no point in doing this piecemeal fundraising exercise for his various projects. It only sucked his energy and concentration away from the actual work. He asked him to take Manish Gupta's help to come back to him with a full-fledged ten-year-plan for what he had in mind for Agastya.

Ramji knew he had hit upon something big and spent the next few months drafting a detailed action plan with Gupta. They went back with a plan that would cost Jhunjhunwala a whopping ₹90 crores over ten years and benefit 6 million children.

"Nobody in India will give you this kind of money,"

Jhunjhunwala said when he heard what they had to say.

A crushed Ramji told him that he was willing to sell his house in Bengaluru to raise money in that case, but he would persist.

It was only then that Jhunjhunwala revealed what he had in mind.

"Look Ramji, I wouldn't ask you to develop a plan and send you back. Selling your home is not going to help you achieve your vision. I can't do 90, but I'll give you ₹50 crores, take it or leave it" he said as both Ramji's and Gupta's jaws dropped.

Journey to Scale

Since 2007, Jhunjhunwala's unstinting generosity became the backbone of Agastya's formidable ambitions, giving it long-term funding to not just expand its mobile outreach and develop an iconic campus, but also establish a myriad other ground-up initiatives to expand reach into the deep, rural hinterland of the country.

Today Agastya's presence on the educational map of India is marked by an amazing collection of pioneering interventions along with its flagship mobile science lab program and the expansive Kuppam campus that has become a cradle of discovery for scores of children from different schools who visit every day as well as for the innovators, teachers and educators who come to the campus from across the globe.

While Jhunjhunwala's money and the subsequent fundraising that Agastya continued to do with other supporters like US-based entrepreneur Desh Deshpande gave Ramji the financial muscle to bring cutting-edge learning facilities to Kuppam and hire an army of dedicated staff to aid his vision, the success of the more efficient mobile lab initiative made him consciously focus on bringing about a series of process-driven innovations that would maximize Agastya's reach through minimal use of resources.

There are numerous examples of what Ramji calls "battlefield innovations" that Agastya has nurtured over the years by keeping its eyes close to the ground. For instance, there are the night community vans that educate parents so that they would be encouraging of their children's schooling ambitions. On one of his visits to a community at night somewhere in Andhra Pradesh, Ramji saw a girl named Vasantha who was teaching remedial classes to three–four kids in the corner of her village. This inspired Agastya to launch 'Operation Vasantha', a program where young girls who have the potential to become community role models are paid a stipend to run evening classes across 600 villages in order to engage school dropouts with fun interactive learning activities which would then lure them back to school.

Some of these ideas came about accidently while others were a consequence of keenly observing the gaps in the system and designing solutions to address them.

For example, there is its 'lab-on-a-bike' program which became an extension of the mobile lab initiative. Ramji found that van drivers were an additional cost and were not being optimally utilized while the instructors were busy teaching the kids. Instructors on the other hand would not agree to drive the vans themselves because it was a status issue. Riding a bike however was not a problem for them. So, he conducted a pilot to see if an instructor could carry a lab in a box which would move from village to village on a bike. This thematic kit which contained a variety of objects to conduct scientific experiments was championed by K. Thiagarajan who had left the corporate world to join Agastya.

The kit was not as extensive or expensive as the lab equipment. The bike was also a more cost-effective means of transport as it required lesser fuel and saved the money that would be spent on the driver. And the program gave Agastya the ability to penetrate deeper into the villages where schools could not support the mobile lab infrastructure. It is today a tremendously successful initiative.

In order to achieve its six-million target, rapid scale-up was important for Agastya and after some brainstorming its team arrived at the idea of hosting science fairs. This would be a cost-effective route to reaching large numbers across schools in a particular area. There was some trepidation about whether anyone would come but at Agastya's first science fair in Kuppam, an astounding 13,000 people turned up.

Today Agastya conducts more than 100 fairs every year across rural and urban Andhra Pradesh and Karnataka including massive ones where as many as 50,000 parents, teachers and students gather on a single day to nourish their imaginations and explore possibilities that they would have never believed existed just by sitting in classrooms.

Like many of its innovations Agastya's science fairs too had been conceived in the cauldron of creative pressure. It was at one such fair in the year 2000 that the revolutionary idea for peer-to-peer learning germinated. Agastya could not gather enough teachers for a fair because of which they had to almost cancel the event. But two young schoolgirls clad in *burkhas* approached the staff while the fair was underway and asked if they could be trained to do the experiments so that they could teach the other kids.

That is when it struck Ramji and his team that in a

country where teacher absenteeism is a chronic problem, children teaching children was a transformative idea. The team went back to the drawing board, deliberated on how Agastya could implement this in the classroom and came up with a design for the 'Young Instructor Leader' (YIL) Program, one of the organization's flagship building blocks today.

Under YIL, bright students across government and semi-government schools who show a special aptitude for science in schools where Agastya intervenes through its mobile labs, are specially trained to develop leadership skills and confidence. They then undertake supplementary teaching for their peers. This not only allows them to retain more of what they learn, unlocking their innate potential, but also reduces teaching barriers for the slow learners who are less inhibited to learn from their own friends. An informal self-assessment study conducted by Agastya on its 1,500 YIL students in Andhra Pradesh revealed that 90 percent of them ended up going to university as opposed to a rural average of 15–20 percent, reflecting how the program's intervention at a crucial stage in their lives benefited them academically.

What is interesting about such interventions by Agastya is that they are supplementary, adding value to the existing system rather than seeking to uproot it. A child gets exposure through the van/bike labs, visits to science centers or the Kuppam campus, or through any of the other initiatives only six–ten times a year from the fourth to the tenth standards. The gaps between these visits are important because it lets Agastya cover a bigger ground and does not threaten the status quo directly which makes teachers and government partners willingly partake in the activity. The spacing also enhances long-term retention, believes Ramji, and is a counter-intuitive approach to the continuous learning and mapping method followed by schools.

All of these innovations have been critical in helping Agastya scale up and grow its footprint cost-effectively. And at the core of its success has been its ability to constantly adapt, yielding a capital-efficient, asset-light, decentralized model of growth that has given it the long-term edge and attracted many supporters.

Former president Dr. A. P. J. Abdul Kalam called Ramji one day to request Agastya to launch two mobile science labs that he would personally pay for from the humanitarian award money that that he had received in Darbhanga, Bihar "to reach the poorest and most backward regions". His successor at the DRDO, Dr. V. K. Aatre, too became an avid supporter of the mobile lab concept and joined Agastya's board.

The Ground-Up Approach

At an organizational level, achieving this level of product and process innovation is not easy, and particularly so when one's operations are so scattered. It requires crafting management strategies that allow the spirit of ingenuity to percolate right through the organization, so that ideas can be sourced from the ground up. Agastya today has 1,400 full-time employees and an additional 400 part-time teachers and it requires each of them to 'think outside the box', an adage that can ring hollow if not backed up by solid institutional processes. So how did Agastya ensure that the imaginative instinct trickled down to the very bottom of the organization?

For starters, Ramji knew he could not be the source for

all creative insights and never shied away from tapping into the collective brainpower of his employees. He says that he "goaded his staff—from the top to the bottom—to be creative, so as to prevent an exponential decay of vision" that most organizations suffer from. *Nayi Soch,* an internal model-making competition, conceived by Agastya COO Sai Chandrasekhar, a former HP vice president, has become a key platform for Agastya instructors to build learning tools for the future. *Sarga Samvad* or creative dialogues with imaginative innovators, led by Ajith Basu, a former architect, has attracted leaders from across the globe who come and share their ideas and innovations.

> Ramji believes that a culture where small groups of people give creative inputs that a large number of others execute "is unlikely to sustain its innovative spirit".

Ramji believes that a culture where small groups of people give creative inputs that a large number of others execute "is unlikely to sustain its innovative spirit". Innovation ought to be ingrained into the DNA of every employee. And he did this by creating feedback loops with the lower-level staff who were fronting his projects and had direct interface with children. This motivated them because their voice was being heard by the most important man in the organization. It also gave Ramji crucial insights that management consultants and office staff would not have been able to offer.

"The guy going out there in the heat and grime knows best, what the problems are and where the potential solutions lie," says Ramji.

Much like the diverse expertise he brought on board

while starting out, he adopted a unique hiring strategy that did not put a premium on expertise or skill, but rather on energy and enthusiasm. "I would tell people, I wanted a BEE (Bachelor of Energy and Enthusiasm) and not a BE (Bachelor of Engineering)," he quips.

Agastya also kept its organizational structure fairly flat. While an operating hierarchy between instructors, senior instructors, center in-charges, regional managers, directors, etc., was maintained, there was a widespread recognition of the fact that the organization's ultimate success depended on the people who were at the frontier. Ramji and his senior managers' cabins remained perpetually open for anyone to walk in and discuss an idea or a problem.

He also encouraged cross-organizational networking by getting people in different geographies to swap jobs for a period. Agastya's employees routinely switch roles with their counterparts in other cities in order to get exposed to different challenges and ideas. This allows them to both learn new things and open blind spots for others.

Finally, most organizations spend abundant resources in planning, but Ramji and his team believed in quick action. They piloted quirky ideas like 'Operation Vasantha' to see if they worked in a particular scenario. If they did, they were quickly replicated, which is how Agastya has continuously enlarged its vision and built the capability of simultaneously running several groundbreaking initiatives. Its evolution as an organization did not stop at running the Kuppam campus, or the mobile science labs, which were featured in The Rockefeller Foundation's Next Century Awards gallery of top 100 global innovations, and is unlikely to remain static as it aspires for an even bigger imprint on the future.

A Larger Ground to Cover

Agastya turned 20 in 2019. What started as an idea for a static creativity campus to foster experiential learning for children in a remote location in Andhra Pradesh has morphed into a widely replicable model that has succeeded in transforming the educational experience of some of the poorest children in the world, and at an extremely low cost. This has been possible mostly due to the organization's ability to constantly adapt and seize new opportunities. And as Ramji stares into the next 20 years, this is exactly what he and his future-oriented team wants to continue to do, i.e., to adapt and adjust Agastya's working model with a focused view on broadening its canvas and touching more lives.

And there are various ways in which he is doing this.

If science was the medium through which Agastya initially funneled its plan for transforming learning, Ramji has now begun thinking of how he can use art or a multi-disciplinary method to take this a step forward. This idea again is an outcome of closely listening to what kids have to say. It was derived from a college girl who told him that she could not remember anything she had learnt in school, except the detailing of how an African village looked, because she had actually made a replica of one for a project. The hands-on experience built an emotional connect for her and helped her retain the memory, which Ramji thinks art can do wonderfully. He is confident that Agastya's new 'design poetics' project which incorporates art and play into its pedagogy and models "will revolutionize the nature and stickiness of children's and teachers' interaction and experience".

"Our focus is on how to think and not what to think.

We are not interested in ensuring everyone becomes a scientist. Art can be an equally effective medium," says Ramji, revealing plans for a Kuppam-like campus with art or spirituality at its core.

In 2018, Agastya also began engaging pre- and primary school children and brainstorming with college students and lecturers to find out how it can amplify its work in colleges. With support forthcoming from the Karnataka higher education department, this is an opportunity for Agastya to step up its reach to a demographic that is most vulnerable to poor education. Ramji is firmly of the belief that India needs entrepreneurial talent to prevent its vast demographic from turning into a curse, where millions of young graduates enter the workforce without skills that would get them a good job.

Agastya's challenge is to address these fissures, and for that, Ramji believes, it needs to scale exponentially from "an organization to a movement". It has developed the intellectual and organizational muscle to be able to do it, but also wants to leverage digital technology far more than it has, in order to build an even bigger outreach. But all of this will require much more time, dedication, resources and money than is currently available.

Ramji has set the stage for the expansion though with a spectacular target. He wishes to raise ₹1,500 crores over the next ten years—five times more than what Agastya has done through the course of its existence. This will be used towards scaling both the mobile education program and investing in new digital learning tools that would really democratize quality education. It might seem untenable to many at this point, but what Agastya set out to do 20 years ago had also seemed unthinkable to many.

For Ramji, such cynicism only brings a sense of déjà vu

all over again, and pushes him harder to get cracking and reach for his dream.

Sutras to Creating, Sustaining and Scaling Innovation:
Business Insights from the Agastya Journey

In its 20-year journey, the Agastya International Foundation has grown to become one of the largest experiments of its kind in creative science education globally, reaching 12 million children. It is also the only organization that has ticked all the seven fundamental principles distilled by us as being necessary to gather a certain critical mass.

Organization	Gap in the Market, Market in the Gap?	Flexible Approach	Customer Centricity	Capital Consciousness	Hiring – Passion over Pedigree	Culture of Innovation	Amplification of Vision
Agastya International Foundation	✓	✓	✓	✓	✓	✓	✓

Gap in the Market, Market in the Gap: In a country as large and complex as India, delivering basic education to the masses has consistently remained a challenge for the government. While substantive improvements have been seen in enrollment rates, major gaps remain in the quality of education imparted to the poor. The public education system is simply not fully equipped to harness a curious, creative, confident young population that can become potent force drivers for innovation and entrepreneurship. Government control of schools makes the task of improving the scenario an onerous one.

Ramji understood that trying to uproot the system to plug these gaps would affect several vested interests and result in a major backlash. It could very likely even be futile. He did not want to intervene via private schools, because that would be exclusionary, and would not really address the problem. So, what he did to circumvent the challenge was position Agastya's learning interventions as supplementary to what was being taught through the school curriculum. By doing this, he could start making a difference, without posing a threat to the existing system. The partnership model where Agastya would give its students exposures six–seven times a year, did not disturb the extant structure, but still brought need-based education aimed at sparking creativity, improving retention rates and bettering learning outcomes to the poorest of the poor.

Flexible Approach: Organizations such as Agastya that have navigated through the teething troubles of starting up and scaled successfully display two clear behaviors. They set precise goals for themselves, and remain persistent about reaching their targets. But they also remain flexible about how they will get there. Agastya has been amazingly lithe in its ability to respond to ground realities and bend with the wind as and when necessary.

Ramji's goal was to radically overhaul the archaic teaching style that often puts children to sleep and induce new creative juices to flow in them. The way he envisioned this was through a large creativity campus. But when he ran out of money to execute that, rather than getting disheartened, he opted for a less capital-intensive route of deploying mobile vans to achieve the same goal.

And ironically, it was this altered trajectory that gave him the scale of impact he desired. The static idea of a campus would have benefited only a small catchment, but putting learning on wheels allowed Agastya to expand its footprint more significantly across thousands of kilometers in India. Similarly, when Agastya realized it could not find enough motivated government teachers, the organization trained children to teach other children, an initiative that later evolved into their 'Young Instructor Leader' program.

It was because Agastya was flexible that its business model took unexpected twists and turns, which in turn ended up becoming important pivots in its growth story. That Agastya has maintained its adaptive intelligence in the face of growth is also because of Ramji's collegial team of multi-skilled leaders including Mahavir, Thiagarajan, Chandrasekhar, Basu and Hariharan, who left lucrative business and corporate careers to be part of an ambitious and idealistic mission.

Customer Centricity: Agastya's mobile learning model takes education to the student rather than waiting for the student to come to the place of learning. Its customer or student centricity extends beyond just wanting to educate children. The distinct mission is to spark curiosity, to change their behavior from 'yes' to 'why', from looking to observing, from passivity to exploration. As such, its programs are designed to keep children fully engaged and develop a lasting interest in learning. The approach is holistic and puts the student at the center of all the initiatives.

Capital Consciousness: Despite being a non-profit, and operating solely on donations, Agastya has put in place a metric that measures cost efficiency very strictly, and makes a concerted effort to get better at it every year. The metric it uses is 'cost per exposure', which is the money spent giving each child an exposure to its laboratories and learning programs. On an average, each exposure lasts for two and a half hours and Agastya directly reaches about 1.5 million children about six–eight times a year (an almost equal number of student exposures happen indirectly through the teachers that Agastya trains). It is important that a child gets the maximum number of exposures per year, but taking children to a creativity campus, a science fair, or a technology center is not cost-effective. It is Agastya's mobile vans which give it the flexibility to increase the number of direct exposures it can give a child, while keeping costs as low as ₹85 per exposure (the cost of an 'Operation Vasantha' exposure is only ₹6). And the costs are being reduced further as Agastya increases the number of indirect exposures through the teachers it trains.

Reckless expansion can be a big drain on a growing organization. Jhunjhunwala's backing had given Ramji ample opportunity to burn his cash injudiciously by replicating the Kuppam model in five other locations or by investing in building more bricks-and-mortar structures. Although

Agastya was conceived as a campus-based model at the beginning, that did not dissuade Ramji from changing his approach midway when he recognized the transformative, low-cost benefits of mobile outreach. Agastya focused on scaling efficiently, remained extremely capital-conscious despite being endowed sufficiently and greenlit ideas that would only reduce costs further, while expanding its reach.

Hiring – Passion over Pedigree: When unconventional ideas are to be executed, Ramji says that hiring "virgin minds that carry no baggage" can be a big advantage. Diversity of experiences and perspective became solid force drivers of innovation at Agastya because it was the non-experts from outside the traditional turf of education that brought in new thinking, allowing Agastya to execute a really different mission.

"Agastya's raison d'etre is to motivate ordinary people to achieve extraordinary things. Many of our employees from rural areas have experienced the oppressive, straitjacket environment of education. They are passionate about setting it right," says Ramji, narrating an insightful discussion with six underprivileged children. To the question "why do you come to Agastya?" the children replied, "because Agastya's science models are fun and a great source of learning". "Okay, I will gift your school a set of Agastya models. Will you still come to Agastya?" "Yes!" the children replied and explained, "because Agastya's teachers are trained to make the models come alive". "Alright," said Ramji, "I will train your teachers to make the models come alive in the classroom. Would you still come to Agastya?" A brief silence was followed by the children saying yes, they would still come. The reason? "Because the Agastya teacher treats us like a friend".

Agastya today has 1,400 full-time employees and an additional 600 part-time teachers. Many of its hires are from villages and/or have studied in Tier 2 and Tier 3 colleges and carry the obvious disadvantage of not having enough exposure. However, they bring with them local wisdom and an emotional connect which is critical to running a decentralized operation spread over many states.

Culture of Innovation It is Agastya's belief that in order to seed innovation into the DNA of an organization, the beginning is always very important. Your mission and its extent, Ramji says, "affects the very software of how far your organization will reach and the work you will do for the next several years". Agastya's larger-than-life mission to spark creativity and curiosity gave it a wide platform to think out of the box and experiment, both of which were critical to building an innovative organization that could challenge the status quo.

But once the mission was articulated it was equally critical to package it attractively so that people within and outside the organization could really imbibe its spirit, believes Ramji.

When Agastya translated its mission to "spark curiosity, nurture creativity and instill confidence" through the spirit of Ah-Aha-Ha-ha, not only teachers, but even children could understand what the organization stood for. This was critical because its success depended entirely on the teacher effectively disseminating the Ah-Aha-Ha-ha experience to students while conducting the experiments.

But some of the other more operational practices that ensure that innovation percolates down through the ranks at Agastya include:

- A flat operating structure that does away with the obvious boundaries and encourages cross-organizational networking between teams and allows people to change their functions and geographies in order to break the monotony of work and expose themselves to new challenges.

- A senior management group open to innovation.

- An open-door policy that eases accessibility to the leader and opens a regular channel of communication between employees and the management.

- An 'act quick, fail fast' policy that allows employees at all levels to pilot their ideas, discard them if they do not work and implement them if they do by putting in more resources. Ramji is of the belief that he cannot be the sole repository of new ideas, and most of Agastya's programs including lab-on-a-bike (a Google Global Impact Challenge winner), *Nayi Soch* and innovation fairs have been brainwaves of its employees who were given the leadership support to develop them.

Amplification of Vision: Agastya's vision remains unchanged—it wants to ignite Indian minds from the bottom up. However there are four ways in which it is expanding the scope of this vision. First, by beginning to explore art and design thinking and not just science as a medium to foster creativity and curiosity. Second, by taking its programs from the school to the college level. Third, by blending its unique brand of hands-on learning with the power of IT. And fourth, by building new, expansive partnerships and collaborations. As Ramji says, "what Agastya stands for, the spirit of Agastya, is vastly important than the organization".

Beyond these sutras of success though, great entrepreneurs often owe some of their achievement to mentors, advisors or angels who in a greater or smaller degree prove invaluable to a founder's success in the long term. In the case of Agastya, Ramji was the yin to Jhunjhunwala's yang. The latter has truly been an equal partner in shaping the course of Agastya's journey.

What comes out from their collaboration is that patience, persistence and commitment are precious virtues for an entrepreneur. Lack of transparency, inability to sustainably generate long-term impact and poorly calibrated business growth plans are said to be the biggest barriers to securing social capital. Merely having a grand vision or a great idea does not cut it. It is quite clear that Jhunjhunwala was continually testing Ramji's conviction over several years, including his ability to endure rejection and his willingness to personally commit to the project before backing him up. But once he did back him, it was with all his might.

And it is undoubtedly this relationship, apart from all the superior practices it has espoused, that has helped catapult Agastya into a different stratosphere today.

The Better India

Good News Is Great news

A few years after Dhimant and Anuradha Parekh started a weekend blog that foraged for positive stories from around the country, they received an elated thank-you note from a school for the deaf in Chennai. A story that they had run on their blog about this particular school had inspired a group of people to drive down all the way from Bengaluru to Chennai to see the place. Impressed with what they saw, they donated ₹3.5 lakhs to the school in a single shot.

A small story on a tiny blog that had a reach of barely a thousand people every month had effected this reward.

It was a big deal! And it taught Dhimant and Anuradha that no matter what anyone said, positivity was power!

•

Bad news is very often good news in the contorted, chaotic business of media which thrives on scandals, crime, natural disasters, epidemics and terrorism to grab audience eyeballs.

It has traditionally been the function of the press to act as a watchdog of society, our public institutions and other powerful forces. George Orwell, the celebrated writer, once fittingly said: "Journalism is printing what someone else does not want printed, everything else is public relations." It points to the media's predisposition towards unsavory and negative happenings.

Study after study has shown that the news has become progressively miserable through the decades, a reality that is instantly evident when one opens the morning newspaper. Stories of war, crime, ecological destruction, political corruption and financial fraud are mostly what dominate headlines, often giving readers an exaggerated dose of negativity. But this relentless pessimism is what apparently sells. An erupting scandal or a tragic misfortune by its very nature stimulates our curiosity and senses and hence we are more prone to picking up a newspaper or watching a channel with a doomsday scenario playing out. A story brimming with optimism, many in the media believe, has few takers.

Or so Dhimant and Anuradha were told.

But defying popular wisdom, this husband-and-wife duo, both media outsiders with engineering backgrounds who met at an MBA program at the Indian School of Business (ISB), started *The Better India* (*TBI*) in 2008—a Bengaluru-based digital media portal dedicated to covering only positive stories from across the country, with a threefold mission—to inform readers, inspire communities and generate large-scale impact.

Aghast at what they read in the papers every morning, the duo, both avid consumers of content, wondered if the lens through which news was being presented could be changed. Could the newspaper bring a smile to your face rather than make you despondent about the world you lived in? "We were certain that in a country of a billion plus, a lot more good was happening than was being covered in the mainstream media," says Dhimant who was firm in his conviction that 'happy news' had a market and could create big impact if packaged correctly.

"Traditional media has done a fantastic job focusing on what is broken. But if you bombard people with problems without giving them a way forward, they just opt out of the conversation. That is terrible for democracy in the long run because you are essentially only telling them what is wrong, without giving them a solution," he adds. "Our initial idea was to start documenting all the good stuff that people were doing, the solutions they were providing to some of the problems we cribbed about."

And it is with this intention that *The Better India* got off the ground, at first as a personal blog to positively reinforce the good that was happening in the world, and provide a counternarrative to the antagonistic worldview espoused by a large section in the media ecosystem. Being Bengaluru-based, Dhimant and Anuradha's ambitions were limited to collecting stories of local initiatives and sharing them on a blog with their friends, family and colleagues.

But nearly a decade hence, *TBI* has transformed from its fledgling avatar into one of the most impactful alternative media companies in the country with a pan-India presence.

It is read by over 50 million people every month in over 120 countries, it has completed two successful rounds of fundraising, boasts of a string of awards in its kitty and has inked lucrative content partnerships with over 100 marquee corporate and media brands that enable it to make money while also creating social impact.

Most creditably, it has emerged as a catalyzing force

for grassroots-level change across multiple domains, using the power of positive storytelling and solutions journalism to inspire communities and generate tangible, measurable impact on the ground by galvanizing readers to do something about a problem they have reported about through calls for action.

"When the conventional wisdom of physics seemed to conflict with an elegant theory of his, Einstein was inclined to question that wisdom rather than his theory, often to have his stubbornness rewarded," wrote Walter Isaacson in *Einstein: His Life and Universe*. The same can be said about Dhimant and Anuradha, two media non-entities, who came in from the outside and defied what was the accepted norm for the longest time to have their stubbornness pay off.

The Power of Positivity

But how did they pull it off? How did a venture that started as a side hobby go on to capture a unique niche in the manic Indian media market?

Initially, *TBI* had a seven-day working week. The duo did their day jobs Monday to Friday and spent the weekends relentlessly chasing stories—of unsung heroes, change makers and innovators. The response they got from their friends and family was tremendous. But bit by bit, through word of mouth, their reach expanded beyond the immediate network of acquaintances. Writers from Delhi, Chennai and other places then began to get in touch asking if they could contribute to the blog, and communities and social entrepreneurs who were shunned by the mainstream press and wanted to have their work featured approached them for coverage.

The growth was purely organic and *TBI* emerged as a singular purveyor of good stories in a media universe hopelessly preoccupied with misery. It was this niche that gave them the leash to capture new territory. But *TBI* continued to remain a weekend endeavor till 2012 when a few big turning points drove Anuradha to quit her job and direct focus on the site full-time.

For starters, the school for the deaf in Chennai got in touch. A few weeks later, a story about a photography club run by the Beyond Sight Foundation for the visually impaired caught the attention of a blind girl. She too told them that the story they had put out had transformed her life. She had always wanted to learn photography but had felt that her dream was out of reach. Now by approaching the foundation for help she had come several steps closer to achieving her goal.

By 2012, such positive feedback began coming in clusters, with more and more people writing in to say how they were inspired to do something because of the stories they had read on *TBI*. At one point, it came to Anuradha's notice that the BBC's Hindi language service had begun picking up their content as leads for their stories, giving both her own organization and the ones they wrote about a global reach.

All of this was a validation of the vision they had set out with. The duo quickly realized that what they had going had tremendous potential to explode into something significant because they had hit the sweet spot by filling a gap that nobody in the otherwise competitive market had yet occupied. If their stories which were reaching barely a few thousand every week were having such an impact, a bigger audience would make them a force to reckon with. The time had come to take a leap of faith and for at least one of them to devote their full might to growing the website.

And so, leaving Dhimant to keep the home fires burning, Anuradha put in her papers to direct her attention solely to *TBI*. It did not take very long for Dhimant to follow suit though. By 2014, without too much effort, half a million people were consuming their content every month and *TBI* was at an inflection point from where it could either soar higher or take a nosedive. And it required more than one person to chip in and ensure the latter did not happen.

The BBC's Hindi language service started picking up their content as leads for their stories, giving both her own organization and the ones they wrote about a global reach.

While the proof of their product lay in the traffic the site was generating, expansion required capital. They were at a point where they needed to hire teams, set up an office, build technology and spruce up the marketing and distribution effort in order to scale. Early conversations with angels were unsettling because without exception Dhimant and Anuradha were told that despite their growing popularity, the media business was not a lucrative space to be in. Competition was intense and opportunities to monetize were few because of a broken subscription model. More than one person advised them to shut the venture down and not put any more money into it.

Not ones to be demoralized, the duo dug into their savings, raised a small amount through friends and family and continued to run the show for the next one year.

Pressing the Right Buttons

But with funding not forthcoming, the duo did not have the luxury for trial and error, which turned out to be a blessing in disguise. This was because unlike well-funded entrepreneurs who could afford to let their idea breathe over time and do multiple iterations, they had to sharpen their focus quickly and put in place a business model that was lean, clear in its purpose and had the capacity to become self-sustaining over time.

The key challenge initially was how to get content from all the corners of the country without investment in a huge team of reporters. To circumvent the problem, Anuradha spent the first few months after quitting her job building a source network of professionals working across social domains, from NGOs to grassroots activists, health workers, stringers and others who could be onboarded as contributors.

Not only did this enhance her own understanding of the work that was happening in areas as wide-ranging as health, education, wildlife conservation, rural affairs and gender rights, but more importantly, created a symbiotic relationship between *TBI* and the social sector. The community got a platform where they could share their positive work and *TBI* got crowdsourced content for which it did not have to shell out any money.

Very deftly, it had exploited a crucial gap that existed between the demand for coverage of such work and the supply of media channels that would allocate space for it. This saved the site newsgathering and HR costs, which are prohibitive for a media start-up without funding, and allowed *TBI* to make do with only a small team to edit and curate the stories that came in from all over the country. It also accelerated the scale up in terms of the number of stories the site could put out every day.

Even today the site works with thousands of external contributors and a small in-house editorial department of 26 people which keeps the overheads—the cost of content generation, salary and administrative expenses—extremely low.

The second important ingredient of *TBI*'s early scale-up success was the timely realization that in a market where subscription revenue was virtually non-existent, it had to move away from the news function of 'informing' people and work towards 'inspiring' them. This shift was necessary in order to expand its reach and impact, and re-engineer itself as a social impact organization rather than a media start-up that no one was interested in funding. One of the simple ways in which *TBI* did this was by giving 'calls to action' at the end of their stories, urging readers to volunteer for or donate money to the organizations that were featured on the site. With this one move they transitioned from being informers to facilitators.

"Initially the idea was to build a knowledge repository, but soon we focused on how to get people involved. We wanted them not just to read our content, applaud and go away, but do something to improve the status quo," says Anuradha.

The decision to bring about this interactivity element worked wonders at many levels. By early 2015, *TBI* raised ₹1 crore through a couple of angels and an impact fund that agreed to come on board purely because of the 'impact' factor rather than the readership reach. The funding agencies liked that they were involved with positive news which made them feel different from the market, and also that they were doing it to drive change and mobilize people to take action rather than as an end to itself.

It was a successful transformation—from a platform for happy news to a solutions-driven outlet that would promote a cross-pollination of ideas. This was a result of both their inability to generate funds as a pure play media start-up and the recognition among the founders that their content need not merely be an end to itself but a catalyst for readers to act upon as changemakers.

"For instance, we had readers who were inspired by a positive story about an initiative in Punjab, replicating the same idea in Chennai, with resounding success," says Dhimant, explaining what exactly this 'cross-pollination' meant and the multiplier effect it had.

From helping farmer widows set up sustainable businesses to lighting up villages with solar lamps, the end outcomes of *TBI*'s stories are well-documented.

In 2013 for instance, it ran a piece on a childcare center run by a 95-year-old in West Bengal which led to many of its readers visiting the place and contributing ₹5 lakhs for the initiative. A report about conservation efforts in a particular hill station grabbed the attention of government authorities who helped influence the policies to aid that effort. A Facebook post about jobs for the specially-abled went viral and readers were able to get eight of these people roles in different companies. A profile on Amit Godse, a man who started Bee Basket Enterprise with a vision to save rare Indian bees killed by pest control treatments, received tremendous response from readers across the country from Manipur to Maharashtra who helped him in his efforts by providing timely information. In 2017, its campaign #FightDrought raised ₹10 lakhs which was given to the Environmentalist Foundation of India to restore rural water bodies.

These are just a few of the many examples of how the site's positive storytelling has spurred readers into action, keeping them from being just passive consumers of its stories. They are also proof of the success its dual 'inform and impact' model of journalism has had in bringing tangible change on the ground.

Metrics are powerful tools. But entrepreneurs often have tunnel vision about which metric to pay attention to and which to ignore. Most journalistic organizations for instance only tend to watch page hits and audience reach as ways of measuring their success. But they do not consider if those are really the most important end goals of their organization.

TBI realized that news cannot be an end in itself. It realized that the real measurement of their success would have to be done by assessing the impact of their stories, an invaluable insight that helped them to pivot from merely wanting to chronicle the good in society to inspiring and enabling others to make a difference. In a sense, it challenged the metrics that journalistic outlets used to measure their purpose and success.

Profit-First

Retaining this momentum without a paying subscriber base was not sustainable in the long run however and the funds *TBI* had raised were not going to last forever. Unlike most social entrepreneurs, Dhimant and Anuradha were not happy depending on donations from the odd patron or impact funds to remain operational. They wanted the venture to became a for-profit, self-sustaining business that would grow on the strength of its own cash flow.

The big question before them in 2015 thus was how to find creative ways to monetize their content and become profitable. Putting up a subscriber pay wall which, apart from being a hugely risky option, was exclusionary in nature and would automatically shut out a large readership that could otherwise benefit from the stories on the site. It would have defied the very purpose of what they were doing. So, the only option was to get advertisers on board.

And it was as a result of these deliberations that *TBI* started co-creating sponsored 'Partner Campaigns'.

> The big question before them in 2015 was how to find creative ways to monetize their content and become profitable.

These were essentially corporate-funded crusades that gelled with the ethos of the website. Their first campaign was with Vodafone, curated around the catchphrase 'Mobile for Good'. It showcased through stories and videos how individuals were using mobile phones to bring social change. For instance, it showed how an application sent SMS reminders to women dwelling in slums to take their vaccinations. This was followed by various other equally high-profile ones such as #DriveSafe India with Maruti Suzuki, and #SkillsToSucceed, a special series in collaboration with Accenture, that showcased the importance of skills-training to improve employment readiness.

"This model worked really well for us because we collaborated with 100 top brands who saw us as a unique platform where meaningful content around their values could be created," says Anuradha. Additionally, the sponsorships gave *TBI* a revenue stream that allowed them to "make money while driving social change, a rare intersection that's not easily arrived at," she adds.

Today, the sponsored campaigns/creative partnerships drive 80 percent of *TBI*'s revenue despite making up only 20 percent of its content flow. From a bottom line perspective, they have allowed *TBI* to scale up rapidly in a matter of just a few years. It broke even a year after raising capital in 2015 and is today profitable on a month-on-month basis, which is noteworthy because it operates in an environment where digital media companies are operating like technological start-ups, guzzling capital even before figuring out how they will make money in a sector where opportunities to monetize are very limited. A significant number of them particularly in the news business are in fact dependent on endowments from organizations like The Independent and Public-Spirited Media Foundation.

"We are consciously growing in proportion of the revenues that we generate and that pace has increased in the last two years. Our model is a profit-first model that works with elementary logic—keep your costs lower than your earnings," says Dhimant, explaining his exceptionally capital-conscious growth strategy. "Right from the beginning we said we are going to keep ourselves lean. We didn't want to bloat up, and a self-imposed scarcity really pushed us to innovate on new content and revenue models."

As a purveyor of feel-good positive stories the very nature of its offering shields *TBI* from nuisance that most media companies face, i.e., an adversarial relationship with brands that can develop as a result of negative coverage around financial transgressions, poor corporate governance or developmental practices, which can then impact advertising revenue. But the founders are mindful of the fact that they will not do PR for the brands they work with. It is a tricky but essential stipulation for preserving their own editorial integrity.

In fact, in order to ensure that there isn't an overreliance on corporate collaborations, *TBI* has over the years begun looking at diversifying its revenue stream as well, which includes content syndication partnerships where its content is used by other portals, licensing of its publishing and audience engagement tools which it has built in-house and consulting on corporate social responsibility (CSR) initiatives undertaken by big corporate entities. There are also plans for an events division and for subscription revenue to begin flowing in through reader donations.

Riding the Technology Wave

Concurrent with these innovations on revenue and content, it is *TBI*'s technology-focused growth strategy that has been the biggest driving force of its scale-up journey. It was quite early in the day that Dhimant, who has an e-commerce and product background and handles the technological side of the operations for the website, realized that while content was king, technology had to be at the heart of the company's expansion plans. Too many outlets out there were engaged in a fierce battle for consumers' attention and simply putting out great stories was not going to make the cut. *TBI* needed to be visible everywhere in order for it to stand out in a sea of websites, newspapers, news channels and social media pages.

Dhimant attributes a big part of their success to this early recognition of the reality that walls between media and technology had to be broken down in order to succeed in a new disruptive environment that put a premium on visibility and virality. *TBI* could not remain just a media company but had to become a technology platform that was in the business of creating content. So, while Anuradha focused on the editorial side of the business, putting her mind to creating disruptive content such as snappy videos, mobile-friendly listicles and creative brand integrations with a capacity to go viral, Dhimant donned the mantle of the technological brain, ensuring that what she created was being disseminated to as many people as possible.

"We were leveraging each other's skills, which were very complementary, and which a lot of media companies didn't tap into, eventually losing out of the game," he says.

Hectic experimentation with various technological platforms, distribution models and a quest to stay ahead of the several waves of digital transformation that hit the media industry during this period helped the site consolidate a strong position amid a flurry of new entrants. An essential metric to measure the success of a portal is its reach, and between 2014 and 2018, in a span of just four years, *TBI* saw exponential growth—half a million to a whopping 35 million readers every month.

Of course, its unique positioning as a solutions journalism platform played a big part in this scale-up, but a deft understanding of the technological side of the business was critical to amassing such massive readership numbers.

But how exactly was *TBI*'s use of technology different from that of its peers in the market?

These were years when Google, Facebook and Twitter had emerged as crucial content distribution platforms and Dhimant did everything he could to draw large traffic from these networks. This meant becoming extremely proactive in customizing its content formats for not just the portal, but also a fragmented ecosystem of social networks, video streaming devices, picture sharing and smart phone applications, GIF formats, etc. Unlike several other media companies offering a one-size-fits-all product, *TBI* proactively responded to the specific needs of each medium differently.

Its unique positioning as a solutions journalism platform played a big part in this scale-up, but a deft understanding of the technological side of the business was critical to amassing such massive readership.

"We consciously began identifying trends early and going all out in devising our strategy accordingly," says Dhimant. "For instance, when we started, we were doing a lot of filter blogging. Then we moved to long form content which only interested people who came from the social impact space but few others. So, we began experimenting with shorter formats and saw more and more people began reading us. We then moved to video content very early, around 2013. Facebook had just started to push video content on their platform, [and] we were ready to do a deep dive."

Today 40 percent of *TBI*'s content is video from just 5 percent a couple of years ago. Similarly, 50 percent of it is tailored for social media and not for the website alone. As a result, its content is present everywhere, giving even those not visiting the URL directly access to its stories.

But remaining at the cutting edge of a digital trend and often second-guessing it means having an appetite for failure as well. And Dhimant and Anuradha always encouraged people to "experiment quickly, fail quickly and roll back quickly, and on repeat mode".

In 2016, for instance, they invested money and time

in creating a "Reddit for good news", modeled on the American social news aggregation platform where people could come and share positive social stories. However, they realized soon after the launch that very few readers wanted to contribute content. Most of them were there just to read it rather than act upon what they read. They had to quickly shut it down. It was one of the first failures the company had, but also became a big learning curve. "We did it on the basis of our own assumptions," admits Dhimant, "instead of studying what the market really wanted".

But as much as it may set you back with failure, experimentation also raises the odds for success. And at the core of *TBI*'s DNA is experimentation, possibly because both Dhimant and Anuradha came from technological backgrounds. "You have to be experimental with a technology product because you don't know what will work, so you ship a product, get feedback and then build on the product again," explains Dhimant, hinting that transporting this trial-and-error approach used by technology companies into the media ecosystem could have been a reason why they have been so successful in some of their experiments.

This includes its pioneering trials over the last couple of years with WhatsApp distribution to scale beyond the duopoly imposed by Facebook and Google. And it shows that the site has not just been able to ride this disruptive digital wave, but also remain ahead of it.

Penetrating the Deep Web

While most native digital news start-ups have over the past five years focused their strategy on piggybacking off Google, Facebook, Twitter and Instagram to drive traffic to their portals, *TBI* realized in 2017 that WhatsApp with its reach of 200 million active Indian users had quickly become the primary communication channel for people. The content being shared on the platform though was largely mindless— good morning messages, funny videos and fake news—and was ripe for disruption. Penetrating the deep web that was WhatsApp could allow *TBI* to circumvent industry-wide concerns about unfair algorithm changes by social networking websites that frequently threatened to restrict publishers' ability to reach audiences, and help consumers to cut through the information clutter and directly read quality content on their personal feed, increasing their proclivity to click.

The team led by Dhimant began an experiment where they circulated a WhatsApp number on *TBI*'s social media pages that subscribers could use to request for content. This would be sent to their screens as a broadcast feed. The response was terrific. Very quickly, one number morphed into two, three, four and five until the phone could no longer support the volley of subscriber requests that began coming in. It also became impossible to feed in this data manually, so the number was abstracted into a URL and the whole process automated, architecting a complex in-house WhatsApp content distribution platform through which video and text could be automatically sent to thousands of subscribers.

Along with this, *TBI* also tried to ensure that the content was actually consumed with as few barriers to access as possible. This meant sharing direct low-resolution video files on WhatsApp that consumed less data rather than a link that would redirect people to a video, or an image with text embedded in it, rather than a URL to an article. The site also built an element of virality into the content by attaching a note that asked non-subscribers keen to receive such content directly on their phones to send them a 'START' message. Through their subscribers' network thus, *TBI* created a link chain of sorts and penetrated the invisible internet.

> *TBI*'s nuanced attention to detail towards distribution and content marketing has resulted in a WhatsApp subscriber base of over 100,000 individuals today, and growing at the rate of 500 additions every day.

This nuanced attention to detail towards distribution and content marketing has resulted in a WhatsApp subscriber base of over one lakh individuals today, and growing at the rate of 500 additions every day, to whom curated stories from the site are sent directly.

The website is a definite first mover in this sphere and is soon planning to license the ingenious tool it built to other businesses which will add to its revenue stream. This strategy also makes *TBI* more attractive to brands wanting to advertise because it is reaching audiences with poor bandwidth and cheap smart phones that cannot access the rest of social media or the internet universe otherwise.

The content delivery and consumption rate (content views) on WhatsApp at 75 percent also far exceeds Facebook and others where only 4–5 percent of the people who like a page end up actually reading/viewing the content that is posted. This makes WhatsApp a much more effective platform of dissemination. And with Facebook's organic reach reducing year by year—down from 5.4 percent in 2015 to 1.2 percent (of a page's subscribers) in 2018 in the Asia Pacific Region according to data compiled by the digital agency Bonsey Jaden—WhatsApp is the future, believes Dhimant, and *TBI* is well-prepared to capitalize on its growth.

An Explosion Awaits

As it completes ten years in business, what is perceptible about *TBI*'s growth trajectory is how all-encompassing its approach to scaling has been. Unlike many media companies that tend to overemphasize one aspect of their operations at the cost of others, *TBI* successfully grew with a holistic focus. It paid equal attention to garnering traffic numbers, generating and documenting impact, turning profitable, growing revenue and innovating with its technological capabilities, the sum total of which has put it in an enviable position to leverage the massive opportunities that lie ahead.

As smartphone penetration in India, fueled by cheap data, sees 15 percent growth year on year, and with more than a quarter of the country's population hooked to these devices, the market for content creators like *TBI* has only just ripened.

While it has already captured 35 million of a total universe of 70–80 million consumers that read and view English content in India, the site is now looking to drive future growth by reorienting its focus on regional content which Dhimant believes is the next logical progression.

"We've already done a soft launch of Hindi, and will be focusing on other vernacular languages over the next few years," he adds. *TBI* is also targeting a fourfold growth in revenues and wants to deepen its reach to 100 million people as a result of this opportunity. "The largest vernacular population right now is on WhatsApp and the way we innovated that sphere will ensure that regional content will work to our advantage."

But the bigger vision for *TBI*, he reveals, is to turn it into a global platform for doing good, which will essentially mean branching out into more avenues than they are already in.

There is another wing under the umbrella of *TBI* that is quickly growing and may soon overtake the media wing. *TBI* wants to create a massive impact on society, and the only way they can do this is by getting everyone involved. How do you do this? Through what they call "responsible commerce".

The premise is simple: people shop for things. There is no denying that. The way to enable people to do good is to leverage this behavior in a brand-new manner. *TBI* is creating the largest aggregation of SMEs, artisans, marginalized communities and sustainability-focused companies that are making unique products. Their approach is two-pronged: circulate income throughout the nation, especially to communities that have great skill but may find it difficult to find business, and promote an overarching environmental consciousness by making available products that help people practice it, through sustainable processes and products made of sustainable materials or by promoting an eco-friendly lifestyle. "In this way, we envision a bootstrapping of society," says Dhimant. "We help bring income to all kinds of communities, which raises their standard, and we are promoting a cleaner environment. All of these elements come together to make a great society. It happens when the individuals within a society are healthy in body and mind, and are placed in a healthy environment."

That is still a long way off from what it is today—an impact-focused positive news platform. But its current avatar too is a universe away from what it once was—a fledgling blog run by two individuals hell-bent on proving to the world that if bad news was good news, good news could be great news.

And boy, have they done that!

Sutras to Creating, Sustaining and
Scaling Innovation:
Business Insights from the *TBI* Journey

The story of *TBI* is in essence one of two 'outsiders' coming in and challenging the status quo with a distinctive product, disregarding set conventional ideas about what can work and what cannot. It is also equally the story of a company that has smartly ridden the technology wave and remained at the cutting edge of the digital disruption to consistently second-guess new trends and remain ahead of the curve with its offering.

These attributes are what have aided its rapid growth from a fledgling blog to a niche alternative media company that has no real competition in the market.

But *TBI* has also firmly adhered to five of the following seven scale-up sutras during this expansion phase.

Organiza-tion	Gap in the Market, Market in the Gap?	Flexible Approach	Customer Centricity	Capital Con-scious-ness	Hiring – Passion over Pedigree	Culture of Innova-tion	Amplifi-cation of Vision
TBI	✓	✓		✓	✓		✓

Gap in the Market, Market in the Gap: The idea for *The Better India* came as a result of the emphatic deficit of good news in the mainstream media. The gap was staring Dhimant and Anuradha, who were avid consumers of news, in the face. But as they began putting resources into the website, they got conflicting feedback about whether there was really a market for such a product. *TBI*'s readers were telling them that they found value in what the site was offering. That was evident from their growing traffic. On the other hand, media insiders and the VC community they were chasing for funding were not convinced that positive news could be monetized.

Such feedback can put entrepreneurs in a quandary. And in such a scenario, the only option before Dhimant and Anuradha was to listen to everyone, but ultimately trust their own guts. They did exactly that—followed their instinct, but remained steadfast in their conviction to prove the naysayers wrong.

Alex Nocifera, a serial entrepreneur who has founded three venture-funded companies, has this to say to entrepreneurs about trusting their instincts: "[When] you're running a start-up—you're officially in the business of disrupting and changing behavior, meaning you're very much at the epicenter of mistakes. If you're waiting for the perfect, no-risk answer, there's a good chance that the opportunity will fly by—sometimes right into your competitors' hands. Embrace the potential of being wrong, but don't be afraid to go with that priceless human instinct."

Dhimant and Anuradha trusted theirs, and thank god for that!

But creating a market for their product was easier said than done. It entailed creating new avenues to generate revenue (such as online media partnerships with corporations) because the subscription model was broken. It also involved a repositioning and transition from being a mere platform for positive news to a solutions-driven outlet that helped people engaged in good causes amplify their impact by giving 'calls to action' at the end of the stories that urged readers to volunteer for or donate money to the organizations featured on the site. This was necessary to attract impact funds that did not want to invest in a pure play media business.

Instead of giving up, or reinventing the proverbial wheel, Dhimant and Anuradha made tweaks and improvements to create a model that addressed the concerns that potential backers had raised about there being a gap but not a market for such a product. It is a great example of using feedback constructively, while not letting it act as a deterrent to one's beliefs.

Flexible Approach: At the core of *TBI*'s DNA is experimentation. The company is in constant trial-and-error mode, and does not have fixated ideas about doing things only in a certain established manner. It is a reflection perhaps of the technology background of the founders. Both Dhimant and Anuradha believe that experimentation and learning from their failures is what makes them different.

On an ongoing basis, they experiment with content types, formats, revenue streams to grow the business and build their community of readers, without diluting the brand and what it stands for. This nimble-footedness is vital for surviving the state of flux that the media industry finds itself in as a result of rapid changes in technology.

"Simple shifts in business strategy or outlook can be every bit as powerful as new technology and groundbreaking discoveries," says Scott Steinberg, author of *Make Change Work For You: 10 Ways to Future-Proof Yourself, Fearlessly Innovate, and Succeed Despite Uncertainty. TBI* has followed this maxim to the hilt, trying continuously to make simple shifts that help it stay up to speed with the changing environment and allow it to "continually reestablish competitive advantage", as Steinberg puts it.

Dhimant and Anuradha passionately believe that while you should have conviction in your vision, "don't persist if things are not working in a certain way—persist with your cause, not the path you take to reach it."

Capital Consciousness: Thrift is your best friend when starting out as an entrepreneur. Overspending can become one of the biggest pitfalls of raising capital because entrepreneurs often discard their frugal ways on the road to success. With no financial backing, Dhimant and Anuradha did not have much of a choice but to squeeze the last drop out of every rupee.

In fact, lack of money was what informed their newsgathering strategy, which has kept *TBI* a lean organization. It works with crowdsourced stories from freelance contributors who share the passion for positive journalism and often send in contributions for free. This model has allowed the company to save on the biggest expense of a media organization—newsgathering and staff salaries. It is one of the main reasons why, unlike many media companies, *TBI* has managed to avoid quick cash burn.

"We are an earn-first, spend-later kind of company," says Dhimant. It is a laudable maxim for a social innovator to live by because the world is broadly divided into non-profits that solve social needs through a donation-based funding model, and for-profit businesses that cater to customer demands through a marketplace model that seeks to maximize bottom lines. There are very few organizations like *TBI* that successfully develop a for-profit social impact business model that falls between these extremes, making it both self-sustaining as well as sustainable in nature.

Hiring – Passion over Pedigree: *TBI* acknowledges that its biggest challenge is to attract the right talent. It has a small team of 16 writers, of whom three are engineers with no writing experience but do so anyway for the love of it.

What makes its recruitment process different from the industry is that it does not believe in focusing on pedigree. It does not look at what the person has been doing but rather their ideas on what *TBI* is doing and their ability to deliver on those. It believes that such people have an ability to take higher risks and fit into *TBI*'s culture of 'try and fail'. *TBI* believes that the willingness to experiment, fail, learn from mistakes and move on is the only thing that can get them big returns and hence the focus is on hiring people who have the right attitude even if not the best aptitude for that role.

Also, most of their content is crowdsourced and written by domain experts working in the social sector, not trained journalists. Their belief is that formal training should not be a barrier to entry for those wishing to come on board as contributors.

Amplification of Vision: Finally, despite its media moorings, *TBI*'s technology-first approach—a result of its founders' technology background—ensured that it saw the world through the lens of great products or platforms. This inverted thinking gave the company a leading edge because it spent time understanding how technology affected both the business and the consumers and quickly engineered strategies to stay ahead of the curve.

Today every company needs to be a technology company, no matter what product or service it provides. Jes Staley, Group Chief Executive of Barclays, once said that he considers his bank as "a technology company with a balance sheet". In a world being disrupted by artificial intelligence (AI) and data, it is companies that use technology for their competitive advantage that are winning the scale-up game. Uber, Amazon, Facebook and Tesla may be transportation, e-commerce, social media and automobile behemoths respectively, but it is their underlying technology that gives them the valuations and edge they command over several others.

TBI too is gearing up for the future from a heavily technology-tinted lens, piloting AI tools to help people do good and attempting a go at building a social network for those wishing to contribute positively among many other things. It wants to evolve into a platform ecosystem for positive impact rather than remain just a media portal. It is a plan that reflects the founders' expanding ambition for the future, and the belief they have in the power of technology and positive interventions to help them grow exponentially from here on.

8

St. Judes

A Crusade against Cancer

In the summer of 2015, doctors told Maruti Mane that his young son Harshal had early-stage blood cancer, a potentially life-threatening disease that had to be treated with utmost urgency if the boy was to be saved. They also dropped another bombshell—the surgery would cost ₹15 lakhs, a figure many times more than the farmer's net worth which consisted of a small dwelling at the far end of a sugarcane field in the grubby little village of Mhaisal in southern Maharashtra.

His best bet, the doctors said, was to take Harshal to Mumbai where institutions such as the Tata Memorial Hospital did such surgeries for free.

For Mane, Mumbai was the proverbial big city from which one never returned. But he shrugged aside his trepidation, got a reference letter from the doctors, accumulated enough money to last a few days and set out for the big journey ahead with Harshal and his grandmother in tow.

The city was all that it had promised to be and more—

big, impatient, unruly and thoroughly intimidating. It took several hours for the diminutive trio to navigate their way to the gates of the Tata Memorial Hospital where after cutting through chaos and crowds Mane got Harshal admitted.

The surgery was a success. For eight days the boy was kept under observation. His grandmother would be allowed to sleep beside him in the room but Mane had to find a place for himself to camp through the night. With nowhere to go, he would kill the time playing a cat-and-mouse game with the staff who persistently shooed away the families of patients crowding the hospital's passages.

On the ninth day, Harshal was discharged. But he was asked to report to the hospital every week over the next six months for chemotherapy. That put Mane in a fix. He neither had the means to travel to and from Mumbai every week nor to rent a room to live in the city.

"We left the hospital and had nowhere to go, but the streets," he says.

Mane and his family had seen crippling poverty all their lives. But nothing had quite prepared them for the indignity of existence on the streets of Mumbai. It was the peak of monsoon, and amid mosquitoes and giant bandicoots, across a swarming garbage dump with an unbearable stench, they spent 25 days on the pavement outside Tata Memorial Hospital. They were witnesses to raging street brawls and the cacophony of vehicle traffic, had barely enough food to eat and piling debts.

Harshal's condition deteriorated rapidly. His immunity was already compromised and he caught a terrible viral infection. Within days, he was also detected with malaria and then chikungunya, a dreadful infection that gave him the most crushing pain in his bones. Mane's world came crashing down. Unable to cope with the successive tragedies and emotional traumas of dealing with the disease, he decided to abandon treatment and go back home.

Fortuitously, only a day later, he met a woman at the hospital who directed him to an address that changed the course of his son's destiny. It was of an organization called St. Judes, a one-of-a-kind shelter that provided thousands of non-affording children such as Harshal a roof over their heads and holistic care during the critical months of their cancer treatment at no cost.

"I could not believe my eyes when I saw the center. I wouldn't have been able to give him the facilities they provided, even in my own home," says Mane, tearing up. "It reaffirmed my belief that there was someone up there looking out for me and my son."

Today, nearly four years later, Harshal is a healthy, happy child in remission. He comes to Mumbai only once every six months for a check-up, but eagerly looks forward to his visits because he gets to go back to his second home, the St. Judes center in Parel, where he reclaimed his life from the clutches of a deadly disease.

A Rash Promise

St. Judes was founded in 2005, on the back of a rash promise when Nihal Kaviratne, a career professional, vowed never to let children like Harshal die of cancer because they could not afford a place to live in during the course of their treatment.

Driving past the Tata Memorial Hospital in Parel in Mumbai one winter morning 14 years ago, Nihal was distressed at the sight of the sheer numbers of visibly sick, bald children sleeping on the pavement outside. These were, he realized, kids from the far-flung corners of India who had come to Mumbai as a last resort to get their dreadful disease treated, but did not have a place to stay in during the protracted course of their chemotherapy or radiation cycles.

Profoundly affected by the sight, he called upon the public relations officer of the Tata Memorial Hospital to check if he could do something about the situation. A few days later, the hospital invited him along with his wife Shyama for a 'Hope Day' function to meet some of the children who were undergoing treatment.

What he saw was a sea of bald, masked faces, sheepishly smiling and interacting with their favorite Bollywood stars, and oblivious to the deadly malady that had afflicted their young lives. Nihal was called up to the dais and a microphone was thrust into his hand. He announced at the spur of the moment that very soon none of the kids present in the room would ever have to spend another night on the pavement or the railway station.

In the 14 years since that audacious promise, St. Judes, which started as one small shelter with eight kids, has gone on to admit over 3,500 children with cancer at its facilities across the country, besides 13,000 returnees during the various stages of their treatment. Its presence has expanded from 1 to 35 facilities with 435 family units, spread across seven cities in India (Hyderabad, Mumbai, Jaipur, Delhi, Kolkata, Vellore and Guwahati), and Nihal wishes to scale up to 100 centers and 1,000 units by 2021. In Mumbai alone, 40 percent of all children with cancer who cannot afford a place to stay are received by St. Judes, and over the years, its intervention has resulted in dramatic improvements in the survival rate of these children.

According to Dr. Rajendra Badwe, director of the Tata

Medical Centre, nearly 30–40 percent of pediatric patients abandoned treatment due to socio-economic compulsions 25 years ago, even though the treatment was free of cost. They were mostly shopkeepers, daily-wage farmers like Mane, or village school teachers who could not afford to sustain the high cost of accommodation in cities, and so, would return to their villages and let the child die.

> In Mumbai alone, 40 percent of all children with cancer who cannot afford a place to stay are received by St. Judes, and over the years, its intervention has resulted in dramatic improvements in the survival rate of these children.

A study conducted by the Boston Consulting Group (BCG) found, however, that as a result of the intervention of St. Judes, the rates of treatment refusal and abandonment had dropped spectacularly from 30 percent to 5 percent at the Tata Memorial Hospital between 2009 and 2011.

In a matter of a decade, this small shelter which was built on a big promise has meaningfully filled a crucial gap in the chain of caregiving in India. It has become a critical node in aiding and sustaining the recovery process of pediatric cancer patients across several parts of the country. It took the vision and determination of one man from the outside to plug a gap that had been visible to everyone in the medical fraternity for years.

A Fateful Homecoming

Nihal Kaviratne was born in Bengaluru to a Sri Lankan aeronautical engineer father and an Indian mother who grew up with roots in Burma. He had a comfortable, cosmopolitan childhood, albeit punctuated with tragedy. He lost his sister to an accident at a very early age in Paris. His mother was a great believer in St. Jude, the patron saint of lost and desperate causes, and spent a lot of her time doing welfare work for needy children, helping out in Catholic orphanages and schools.

Nihal's wife Shyama also came from a family deeply devoted to the cause of the underprivileged. Her grandmother who was based in Bombay had started a school called Bal Anand for street children under a big banyan tree in their house in Malabar Hill.

The couple were evidently greatly influenced by their philanthropic family backgrounds, and very early on in their lives began dedicating some of their time to doing social work.

One day, when Nihal returned home from his travels sometime in the mid-1980s, he found a dozen street kids peacefully sleeping on the floor of his South Mumbai apartment. Shyama had brought them in as it was raining outside. In winters, the couple would buy stacks of warm blankets and roam the streets of Mumbai at midnight, handing them out to shivering homeless children. Even during their 22-year stint abroad, in response to advertisements for funds in newspapers, they would send small checks to charities working for cancer-afflicted children in India. Thus empathy came naturally to both of them.

So, by the time Nihal was nearing his retirement as CEO of Unilever Indonesia, after an illustrious career spanning 40 years (during the course of which he held a series of very senior positions across Asia, Europe and Latin America), the couple was itching to do something more substantial in the social sector. And so, they decided that Nihal would only accept non-executive positions on a few corporate boards, and both he and Shyama would dedicate the better part of their time to philanthropy back in India.

In 2005, they returned home after Nihal's stint in Indonesia. A few days later, the sight of those distressed bald kids on the pavement outside the Tata Memorial Hospital gave Nihal the instant idea to devote himself to a space where work desperately needed to be done.

He was very sure that he wanted to work with kids but did not want to replicate what other charities were already doing. Having donated regularly to the Cancer Aid & Research Foundation (CARF) run by the late Prof. Kazi in Mumbai, he called upon the man to discuss his plans and assess the need of the market.

What Nihal heard from Professor Kazi only further corroborated his suspicion.

The five charities in Bombay working with cancer patients including CARF were only engaged in fundraising for the treatment, and had not quite given a thought to creating a supportive ecosystem and post-treatment infrastructure for the patients. There was a pressing requirement for a facility that would house financially weak, migrant pediatric patients, so that they would not abandon treatment midway.

An intervention was needed without delay.

Think Big, Start Small, Move Fast

A sense of urgency gripped Nihal as he learnt more and more about this dangerous void. He wasted no further time in launching the first center in Mumbai.

"The St. Judes team held its first meeting on February 7, 2006, and by March 31, in under two months, we were operational at the Mhaskar Hospital building in the BDD Chawl area of Lower Parel," he informs.

How did he manage such a quick turnaround?

In return for his presence on the board of a charity run by Julio Ribeiro, the famous former police commissioner of Mumbai, Nihal was given a small space in Lower Parel rent-free. And while that was a big deal in itself, the early days at St. Judes were tough to say the least.

Getting the first eight patient families to agree to leave the street and come to the shelter was a massive challenge. These families had been regularly cheated and robbed of their belongings, and were very circumspect about the proposal to go and live in a place that asked them for nothing in return. Nihal, Shyama and Gargi Mashruwala, who is now the vice chairperson at St. Judes, would go on the rounds personally, wading through knee-deep water in order to convince families in the peak of the Mumbai monsoon when they were at their most vulnerable.

"Today we have the parents of the patients wearing their St. Judes t-shirts, who go out looking for other kids," says Nihal. "It is part of the *kar-seva* concept that we've introduced, inspired by the Golden Temple in Amritsar, where we urge them to give back to society. But back in the day, it was us doing the job."

The duo had razor-sharp focus right from the start and

were willing to go to any extent to get the work done. This can be credited to their abiding interest in the field of children's welfare several years before they decided to get fully involved in philanthropy. But it is to their credit that despite every well-wisher telling them that their idea was crazy, they stuck to their guns and persisted with the plan.

"People told us we wouldn't get free space, but we got that. Then they said, you won't get volunteers, but we got those. Through my 40 years at Unilever, and the 14 years since, if my wife and I've decided to do something, then there's no hurdle around which we haven't found our way," says Nihal who put in his entire final year's salary from Unilever to get the project off the ground.

Apart from putting his money where his mouth was, an important reason for St. Judes' early success was that Nihal and Shyama managed to narrow down their effort very sharply on a gap where they would not be bogged down by their lack of credentials as medical practitioners.

"If I couldn't intervene as a doctor, I had to find a way to be of help from the outside," says Nihal. "And I couldn't bear to see the fruitlessness of the effort put in by doctors in treating these kids, because it was being robbed by infections on the street."

Carving a niche on the periphery of the problem, and making a value addition to, rather than duplicating the effort made by hospitals and other charities, gave them the ability to quickly scale beyond pilot and generate maximum impact in a minimum amount of time.

Early Triumphs

There were a host of other early innovations that gave them the early gains.

Nihal had a well-crafted execution plan concocted at Unilever Indonesia that he put to use while starting St. Judes.

The mantra was 'Think Big, Start Small, Move Fast'. St. Judes started with barely eight family units in a location that was less than desirable, but rapidly worked towards achieving critical mass by a trial-and-error method before templatizing a replicable model that could give it scale quickly.

> Despite Nihal's well-networked, influential corporate profile, St. Judes entirely avoided the traditional, resource-intensive route of hosting gala events or charity dinners to raise money.

"We started the organization by putting in our own personal funds, and spent the first 22 months prototyping everything, from the look and feel of each center, to the governing rules, the selection criteria and modes of intervention—to ensure that they will encompass physical care and emotional development too," says Nihal. "The result of which can be seen in the consistency and standardization across all our centers today."

The duo clearly communicated early on to all their volunteers—all part of their immediate network of friends and family—that they did not want their money, or want them to ask their friends for it. What they wanted was their participation, time and effort so that they could quickly 'show' rather than 'tell' others about the work they were doing. This they believed was a more credible way of raising funds sustainably than asking people to contribute monetarily on the basis of trust or assurances.

Despite Nihal's well-networked, influential corporate profile, thus, St. Judes entirely avoided the traditional, resource-intensive route of hosting gala events or charity dinners to raise money. This is why it comes as no surprise that they have managed to put a cap on their administrative costs at six percent of the revenue generated, making them possibly one of the most cost-effective charities in the space.

One of things that disturbed Nihal greatly about other charities was how high their administrative expenses were. They spent roughly 40 percent on administration and paperwork, which meant relatively little was going towards addressing the actual problem at hand. He decided to tackle this problem by upturning the archaic management pyramid that governed charity organizations, getting rid of a hierarchical 'command and control' operating structure and forming a democratic team of volunteers (rather than paid staff members) who would self-organize to get things done.

It was an interesting inversion of the regular practice at non-profits where volunteers were hired mostly for 'junior' tasks while positions of responsibility were held by paid employees. At St. Judes, the staff would form only a small part of the execution team while volunteers—lawyers, accountants, doctors, administrators and architects who were part of Nihal's influential network of social contacts— would essentially run the show as team leaders, which kept the costs down significantly.

"We started with 16 volunteers, and put out cards on the

table with headings such as fund raising, communications, finance and compliance, operations etc. People put their name beside a role that interested them, and the teams got to work without inter-dependability. Each of them would have a team leader elected by the team itself, and get the job done without any organizational structure in place. People organized themselves," says Nihal.

A strong emphasis was also laid on quality as opposed to quantity when it came to hiring and Nihal had a strikingly unique approach to talent acquisition.

St. Judes would get one competent person to do the job and pay them three times the market rate rather than hiring five inexperienced hands. It was a lesson derived from the Singapore model of staffing public servants where judges, bureaucrats and the police were very highly paid in order to derive high efficiency and root out the temptation for bribery and corruption.

Nihal also introduced, what might have seemed to many, bizarre key performance indicators (KPIs) for volunteers. One of these was that they had to be a chain of people who were third-generation friends with diverse skill sets and jobs that would not transfer them to other cities.

"If a relationship between two friends or families lasts for three generations, it is a bit like love. And while you don't need to be friends to work together, you certainly need to be friends to win together," explains Nihal.

No wonder then that the rate of attrition at St. Judes has consistently remained under 10 percent through the years. Out of the 200 people who work for the organization today, over a half are volunteers and many of them have been around right since inception.

Much else, however, has changed from the days when operations began at the ramshackle chawl in Lower Parel.

The Three Circles

An avenue of dreadfully dilapidated buildings leads to St. Judes's brand new flagship state-of-the-art campus in Cotton Green in Mumbai. On site are a bunch of cheerful kids playing on the jungle gym, screeching and laughing as their mothers try and get them in control while the fathers practice a flash mob in the garden for an upcoming event.

The contrast between the rundown surroundings and the 1.2-acre campus is stark, and in many senses a metaphor for the sign of hope it represents today in a sea of despondency. The center became operational in 2015 after the Mumbai Port Trust in agreement with the Tata Memorial Centre provided the space absolutely free of cost in recognition of the amazing work they had been doing for nearly a decade by then.

St. Judes raised funds from other corporate donors to fully refurbish the place which has today become its largest facility in the country, accommodating 165 patient families and ten doctors.

The positive vibe inside the center is hard to miss. Bright colorful walls, well-lit, vibrant corridors, family rooms with clean curtains and bedspreads, a common kitchen and immaculately sparkling bathrooms are evidence of the discipline with which the center is run. There are handbooks and manuals with detailed instructions and codes of conduct that have to be adhered to strictly.

"No matter which of our centers you visit in the country, they all look exactly the same," says Usha Banerji, CEO of St. Judes, explaining the efforts they have made towards standardizing not just the look and feel of all the 35 centers, but also the key working practices in order to maintain a high degree of uniformity across all their operations.

Owing perhaps to his strong MNC background, Nihal was always of the belief that a shared template of operations can be a strong driver for transformation. This is why he created a three-circled operating structure based on which the day-to-day operations of all the St. Judes centers across the country are executed.

The first circle is the medical/surgical aspect of care. Here, St. Judes works to identify the needs of the patient (admitting only poor patients who come from the hinterland) and the capability of the hospital. If the hospital's protocol insists upon inpatient treatment, it does not intervene. If, however, a hospital requires daycare and housing support, it does a tie-up so as to free up beds and give patients a shelter.

"We get the hospital to also do the due diligence, which requires that they send us only those patients who are treated free of cost, and have at least a 70 percent chance of survival through management of the disease. We take only from this quadrant," explains Nihal.

The second and third circles are the physical and emotional aspects of caregiving. While the second circle is the structured and concrete part of providing families with nutrition and a clean and safe place to live in, the third circle is the more intangible support that is extended through education, recreation and counseling, and a host of parent-centric activities such as vocational skilling.

"For instance, we enroll the fathers into classes at a local car garage, or teach them plumbing, while the moms are taught how to weave baskets," explains Banerji. "Most of our parents are daily-wage laborers on farms or engaged in doing other menial jobs, and these skills can go a long way in giving them other means of employment once they go back."

The plan initially was to extend the scope of its

intervention only to the second circle. But very soon, the team realized that they could not care for the body or the physical well-being of a patient without caring for their mind or their emotional health.

So, these three circles now interlock to form the holistic St. Judes model which successfully works to not just reduce treatment abandonment cases but also instill a positive attitude in patients towards fighting the disease.

"It also impacts the parents profoundly," says Shyama Kaviratne, "at the level of the individual, at the level of the family, and at the level of the community."

> When a new center is set up, 50 percent of the occupants along with half of the staff move from an earlier center to the new one to foster learning among the new occupants.

The nurturing and the quantum change in the environment helps parents overcome the fears of the big city and gives them a renewed sense of hope and energy to concentrate on the disease. At the family and community level, the sharing of tasks with other families—right from cooking alongside and sharing food with a diverse mix of people from all castes and religions to practicing self-discipline in terms of hygiene or alcohol or tobacco use—goes a long way in bringing about communal harmony and a greater tolerance for each other's faiths and beliefs.

In fact, in order to ensure that a sense of community is consistently maintained, parent participation is encouraged. Families are actively involved in the running of the centers and when a new center is set up, 50 percent of the occupants along with half of the staff move from an earlier center to the new one to foster learning among the new occupants.

Despite the three-circled structure providing a broad guide, St. Judes continually evaluates what is working and what is not and there is a steady evolution of practices to keep things flexible and updated.

"For instance, when we began, centers were required to be strictly vegetarian; even eggs could be eaten only in the garden. However, when we opened a center in Kolkata, we realized that this was not feasible and had to allow fish to be consumed as it was their staple diet," says Nihal, explaining the 'learn-as-you-go' approach to growth the organization has espoused through the years.

The Road to 100 Percent

As it approaches 2021, the year for its ambitious '100 centers, 1,000 units' target, St. Judes is in a hectic expansion mode, opening new facilities in Chennai, Vizag, Chandigarh, Lucknow and Varanasi. It is also on the verge of expanding the Kharghar facility in Navi Mumbai. All of this is with a view to providing every one of the 45,000-odd kids in India affected by cancer every year a shot at life.

It is a lofty aim, but Nihal is confident of being able to traverse the journey from 40 percent to 100 percent in the next few years in Mumbai.

"We are run like a company, and we also set targets like one," he says.

Funding is not an insurmountable hurdle for the organization which has, despite its initial reservations about asking for money, managed to garner enough donor support through the years. That is reflected in its annual budget of around ₹20 crores. In 2017, it was awarded a 1B rating by CRISIL for 'strong delivery capability and high financial proficiency', possibly as a result of its efficient operating model that works on procuring real estate space at zero or nominal cost and using donor funds for capital and operating expenditure, which generates maximum impact per penny.

All its accounts are open for audit for big donors like the Tatas and also the nearly 300 other donors who can choose to give from a bouquet of structured endowment options. They also each get a relationship manager who regularly sends updates and progress reports on how their money is being utilized.

Such transparency and resourcefulness have ensured that the organization has a steady stream of corporate and individual benefactors always ready to back its ambitious expansion plans. In fact, many of them are put on a waiting list because St. Judes generally needs its three other requirements—the tie-ups with the right hospital, an optimal space for the shelter and volunteers and staff to run the operations and take care of the patients' emotional needs—to be met before pouring funds into opening a new facility.

While this calibrated approach to expansion has resulted in growth that is sustainable over the long run, the big challenge Nihal expects as they get bigger is to not let these standards get diluted.

"The challenge is showing ourselves and not others that we will not compromise one iota of the established model," says Nihal, who continually confronts the dilemma between expanding rapidly and maintaining a certain quality or standard of operations.

There is also a legitimate temptation to broaden the compass beyond cancer, but with enough work still to be done, a conscious decision has been made to keep the focus steady on cancer till more scale is achieved. "There may be occasions when we find something very close in protocol, for instance Thalassemia, where the line of treatment is very similar to the treatment for blood cancer. We may look at that on an experimental basis but we are still not convinced," says Nihal.

Another intellectual battle at St. Judes today is between sticking to its traditional ethos of not overtly seeking donations and creating a sizable endowment corpus that will afford it some sustainability for the future. While many in the organization feel that a corpus will allow for long-term security and planning, Nihal belongs to the school of thought which believes that it will lead to greater inefficiency.

"The understanding that we have reached is we should have enough money in what we call as the sustainability fund rather than as the corpus. In order to see through every child that we have taken responsibility for so far and that works out to roughly three years of funding," says Nihal.

A Self-Sustaining Wheel

With the organization that they once seeded blossoming, Nihal and Shyama no longer partake in its day-to-day running. In the beginning, Nihal had told his team that he wanted to be out of the board within three years and he has kept his word, instituting a mechanism whereby the chairman changes every three years, giving St. Judes fresh leadership.

While he is still associated as a mentor and meets with his core team every six months to strategize and brainstorm about new ideas, he does not micromanage decisions. For several years, a well-equipped leadership team has been entrusted with the responsibility of running the show. It is a hands-off management style he learnt at Unilever, which is coming in handy as the organization expands its geographical reach.

It is this ability to step back as much as the capacity to be hands-on when required that has fostered a sustained culture of innovation at St. Judes.

From a fledgling eight-family center in a Mumbai chawl to a multi-city chain across the length and breadth of India, the story of this organization is one where the best management practices have merged with the big-hearted desire to give back to society. It is a story of dreaming about change and making that change happen by, as Nihal says, "systematically hammering away at the canvas one chooses."

His straightforward advice to those keen to make a difference but unable to decide what it is that they exactly want to focus their energies on is worthy of attention

"There are only six–seven needs that have not changed through the course of history," says Nihal. "It is the manifestation of these needs that has changed over the years, so smallpox and polio have given way to HIV and cancer. But health, for instance, is a need which has remained exactly the same. Pick one of these six–seven basic needs and look for what the manifestation of that need will be tomorrow rather than today or yesterday—choose to tackle diabetes instead of HIV for instance. And once you have done that look for a gap within that sphere and then go for it full steam."

It is simple, but invaluable counsel on how to sharpen one's interest and capture a niche to generate maximum impact. It is what has powered the growth of St. Judes over the last decade and half, and it is what will possibly drive the organization's future trajectory as well, as it goes from being the biggest chain of shelters for pediatric cancer patients to conceivably the go-to shelter for underprivileged children suffering from all kinds of other deadly diseases as well.

Sutras to Creating, Sustaining and Scaling Innovation:
Business Insights from the St. Judes Journey

From one child to 40 percent of all underprivileged children that come to Mumbai for cancer treatment, and from one center in one city to 35 centers across seven cities in the country, St. Judes's focused expansion has today made a significant dent in aiding recovery among India's most disadvantaged pediatric cancer patients, hugely improving their chances of surviving the disease.

Its growth has been a result of categorically embracing at least four of the seven sutras or principles of scale distilled by us.

Organization	Gap in the Market, Market in the Gap?	Flexible Approach	Customer Centricity	Capital Consciousness	Hiring – Passion over Pedigree	Culture of Innovation	Amplification of Vision
St. Judes		✓	✓	✓	✓		

Flexible Approach: St. Judes constantly evaluates its model to see if it is working optimally and adapts it to suit new environments and situations as and when needed.

For instance, in the early days, St. Judes insisted that both parents accompany their child at the center. But with time they learnt that this was not always possible as it often meant a complete stoppage of income for the family and tweaked the rule to 'two able-bodied adults'. Similarly, keeping geographical, cultural and social sensitivities in mind, concessions are often made regarding food choices, for instance.

This is done without losing sight of its core vision. So, each of its centers is built to uncompromising standards with quality and attention to detail as its mantras. There are manuals for everything at the center from the color of the walls to the food served and the rules to be followed by the parents. These standardized norms are not however carved in stone. They are continuously evolving and responding to dynamic situations.

Customer Centricity: At a time when all other cancer charities focused exclusively on donating for treatment, St. Judes's big triumph lay in recognizing the dangerous gaps in the transitional care ecosystem which often rendered the excellent treatment given by doctors useless, preventing them from serving their patient (customer) optimally. Its sharp focus on post-treatment care to arrest abandonment and improve survival outcomes is a great illustration of holistic customer focus.

While other organizations, or even the medical ecosystem put treatment/operative procedures at the center of cancer care, St. Judes broadened the definition of what 'treatment' meant. It can be thought of as an after-sales service. What is the use of a great product if you cannot get it serviced reliably in order for it to function properly? Similarly, what is the use of aggressive chemotherapy or radiation if compromised immunity as a result of infections, and lack of nutrition, physical and emotional support are going to compromise its efficacy?

St. Judes also addressed the customer centricity aspect through excellent attention to detail. It realized early on that in order to ensure that children do not abandon treatment, the organization would need to focus on more than just meeting their basic needs of food and shelter. Instead of a myopic view of the obvious 'customer' needs, they delved deeper to understand what other things the children needed. Providing those additional requirements, they realized, would urge the children to stay on and complete their treatment cycle. This enabled them to implement several little practices such as:

- Providing personalized, nutritious food to each child that reminded them of their own home.

- Ensuring that the child's educational needs were met even while he was away from home by getting staff members to cover the school syllabus so as to cause least disruption to the routine.

- Ensuring the well-being of the child's parents who stay at the center by giving them skills training or odd jobs, so that they do not disrupt the treatment.

It is these little overlooked details that brought about big behavioral shifts in the families' attitudes towards their children's treatment. The success of this customer-centric approach is reflected in the treatment abandonment rates at the Tata Memorial Hospital which have gone down from 30 percent to 5 percent.

Capital Consciousness: St. Judes is conscious of not only how it raises funds but also how it utilizes them. And it demonstrates its conservative attitude with money in multiple ways. It avoids resource-intensive fundraisers, a norm with most non-profits. Its 'inverted' team structure relies upon volunteers executing high skill jobs and paid staff doing routine work. This keeps personnel costs down significantly. The savings are further aided by its staffing policy which is hinged upon hiring fewer highly-paid but efficient employees rather than several low-paid but incompetent ones. It is no surprise then that its administrative/operating expenses are enviably lower (6 percent as opposed to 25–70 percent) than that of many social organizations.

Also, unlike most other non-profits that raise funds first and then start a project, St. Judes built its first few centers and raised funds on the strength of its offering. This has allowed it to develop a unique approach of showing rather than telling to fundraising. The expectation is that when people visit a St. Judes center, they are so impressed with what they see that they automatically ask how they can contribute.

Nihal believes that the proof of one's worth is in the pudding and that money will automatically follow if there is an inherent value to the work one is doing. This is exactly what has happened. Today St. Judes often has donors on a waiting list!

Hiring – Passion over Pedigree: When the idea for St. Judes was conceived in 2006, the founder got a group of 16 like-minded people together. Each had a different set of skills, but all had one thing in common—a burning passion to improve the lives of children suffering from cancer. Each of these people was assigned an area of work. They were asked to choose what they were 'interested' in doing rather than what they were 'qualified' to do. If they wished to switch roles after a few years and explore a new domain, they were given the freedom to explore that as well.

What happened as a result was that people organized themselves, rather than having to be organized into a pre-determined structure where they felt trapped. This HR philosophy was inspired by practices at Unilever where Nihal spent numerous years. "Unilever worked as a flotilla of ships rather than one big ship and that is why the strength of local companies like Hindustan Unilever could be exploited. They were allowed the freedom and trust to manage themselves," explains Nihal.

His CSR work at Unilever also taught Nihal another key lesson—if you want to bring about attitudinal change, you must bring about behavioral change, and if you want behavior to change, you should first change the existing environment! The St. Judes centers are designed to provide a 'quantum change' in the environment from what the children are used to back home in order to ensure that they run the full length of their treatment and come back for check-ups as well.

It is undoubtedly this ability to effect 'quantum

change' that has propelled St. Judes to take such quantum leaps in its journey thus far.

change' that has propelled St. Judes to take such quantum leaps in its journey thus far.

Acknowledgements

The great paradox of writing a non-fiction book of this kind is that the process is as communal and collaborative as it is private and solitary. On this ride, fraught with agony and ecstasy in equal measure, I could have suffered cognitive dissonance. But a host of people ensured that I did not. To them I owe a debt of gratitude.

Among them are Priya Kapadia and her amazing team at Marico Innovation Foundation who showed unwavering support and direction; the wonderful Nupur Joshi who was always prompt, considerate and the reassuring voice of sanity when things got bumpy; my commissioning editor Reena Jayswal who approached me to write this book, and whose sharp editorial inputs and incisive feedback greatly contributed to strengthening the narrative; the entire support team at Jaico Publishing House; R. Gopalakrishnan whose invaluable editorial suggestions helped me steer the ship straight when it was going off course; all the incredible men and women featured in the book and their communication staff who facilitated my interactions with them. I wish to thank them for their time and cooperation, and for letting me into their worlds.

And last but not the least, my parents, family and friends for being the pillars of support that I could always rely on.